I0786252

ISBN-13:
978-1724529213

ISBN-10:
1724529218

Copyright © 2013, 2014, and 2018 Todd Kachinski
Third Edition

DRAG411's Ten Black Books

Book 1:	**DRAG411's "DRAG Bully, A Survivor's Guide"**
	Copyright © 2015 and 2018
Book 2:	**DRAG411's "Original DRAG Handbook"**
	Copyright © 2010, 2011, 2012, 2014, and 2018
Book 3:	**DRAG411's "Crown Me! Winning Pageants"**
	Copyright © 2013, 2014, and 2018
Book 4:	**DRAG411's "DRAG King Guide"**
	Copyright © 2014 and 2018
Book 5:	**DRAG411's "DRAG Stories"**
	Copyright © 2011, 2014, and 2018
Book 6:	**DRAG411's "DRAG Mother, DRAG Father"**
	Copyright © 2012, 2014, and 2018
Book 7:	**DRAG411's "SPOTLIGHT TODAY"**
	Copyright © 2012 and 2018
Book 8:	**DRAG411's "DRAG Queen Guide"**
	Copyright © 2014 and 2018
Book 9:	Two Comedy Scripts:
	DRAG411's "Best Said Dead"
	Copyright © 2011, 2014, and 2018
	"Following Wynter"
	Copyright © 2012, 2014, and 2018
Book 10:	**DRAG411's "DRAG World"**
	Copyright © 2012 and 2018

From the best-selling author of "CommUnity of Transition,"
"Two Days Past Dead," The Novel and the sequel,
"Turn Around Bright Eyes, The DRAG Queen Killer,"
"Joey Brooks, The Show Must Go On,"
And "Waiting On God."

DRAG411's

Crown Me!
Winning Pageants

3rd Edition

I am not a fan of the term "drag" as applied across this entire art form, but until they find a single word "more accepting," I will have to use it. The drag community has helped me earn twenty LGBT world records. I created DRAG411 to document this form of entertainment. We are the world's largest organization for male, female, and androgynous impersonators with over 7,000 current or former impersonators in 32 countries.   The Infamous Todd Kachinski Kottmeier

Latin adverb: thus"; in full: sic erat scriptum, thus was it written indicates DRAG411 transcribed the comments into this book exactly as found in the original source, complete with any erroneous or archaic spelling or other nonstandard presentation. We try to print the responses using the same words sent to us, ensuring the reader DRAG411 did not change the tone, reflection, or character of each response.

We print verbatim, without editing
ver·ba·tim   vər'bātəm/
adverb: verbatim; adjective
in exactly the same words as used originally.

(sic)

Go to our website at
Drag411.com
to locate any name listed
in any of the books
in our Ten Black Book series
and the details of each
book, entertainer,
and chapter.

Crown Me!

____

Paying It Forward

**"It is one of the beautiful compensations in this life
that no one can sincerely try to help another
without helping himself."**

Ralph Waldo Emerson

~

The Forward

This was supposed to be "a no brainer" book inspired by a comment from drag guru Bob Taylor. Mr. Taylor constantly says, "Someone should tell these performers they are doing it wrong."

Okay, this is I paraphrasing a complicated issue. Bob was addressing those in the drag community that consider him a mentor. I begged him to create an advanced guidebook for drag, but his extensive schedule prohibited his full time attention to my suggested project.

The great benefit of me being the self proclaimed "Nation's Original Drag Historian," is the knowing our database from publishing a host of books and magazines, afforded us the contact information to reach out to over five thousand performers in thirty countries. I knew I could rely on Bob Taylor for a fourteen-question interview, but now I could apply the same set of questions to over four hundred State and National crown holders, along with both pageant system promoters and judges.

Seemed simple; a no brainer.

Every book is a good deed, completed by the hearts, spirit, and wisdom of impersonators trying to help me fill the shopping shelves of HIV/AIDS families struggling to find food in a nation of plenty. Hundreds of crown holders and pageant systems refused to be part of this book. They used words like "You need to compensate me from the food earnings to participate," "I only do HIV related charities, and hunger is not an HIV issue," or "I can't find twenty minutes in my schedule in the next two months to be reply to even one of the fourteen questions." Many more just decided to consider us spam and did not reply at all.

So much for a no brainer.

The drama of the drag dressing room had once again attacked another charitable cause. I wanted to scream, shout, throw a fit in anger, but something happened the following day as my friends began sending in their replies to the questions. They reminded me the best of being "of class" comes from your heart and not just the crown placed upon your head.

Read their advice, one person at a time, each contributing their fourteen unedited replies to create fifteen chapters. Fifteen chapters of the most incredible people in the craft of impersonation, using their skill set, their lessons, showing you the path to succeed; to succeed not only as a competitor for pageants and contests, but also for each time you walk upon a stage.

Never should a spotlight shine upon you, that you do not give each person in the audience the best of every ounce of your spirit, talent, and pride. I thank these performers for showing the same respect for their craft in creating this first ever, groundbreaking book on winning.

The Infamous Todd Kachinski Kottmeier
DRAG411, founder
Infamoustodd.com

We dedicate this book to all the performers
no longer alive to share their wisdom.
Now they each perform now on a
grander stage. Their influence
shines in each spotlight,
lives in each beat, and
felt in each heart.
~

**"I touch the future,
I teach."**

Christa McAuliffe

Contributing Writers

Meet the teachers, the mentors, the friends that opened
their hearts, to share their knowledge with you.
Listed Alphabetically

AJ Menendez
Mister Boiling Point 2009 to current
Mister St. Augustine Pride 2012
Mister Savannah Pride 2010
Mister Florida Ultimate Illusionist MI 2010
Mister Rainbow House 2012
Mister Riot 2012
Mister Lake City Pride 2012

Amy Demilo
Florida Miss US of A 1980
East Coast All American Goddess 2012
Miss Gaybor 2012
Miss Gay USofA Classic 2013

Anastacia Dupree
Miss International Newcomer 2011

Anson Reign
Mister Nebraska USofA MI 2011
Mister King of the Desert USofA Emeritus MI 2008
Mister Arizona USofA MI 2009
Mister Southern States USofA MI 2010
Mister Nebraska USofA MI 2011
Master Male Illusionist First Alternate 2012

Bob Taylor
Judge US of A
Bob Taylor inspired this handbook

Breonna Tenae
Miss SC Gay Pride 1999
Miss Myrtle Beach Pride 1998

Brittany T Moore
Miss Music City AAG 2011
All American Goddess 2013
Ms Heart of Florida 2013
Ms Atlanta Showgirl 2013

Coco Montrese
Miss Gay America 2010

Dana Douglas
Miss Florida 1982
Miss Continental 1987
Miss Universe 1991
Miss Continental Elite 2012

Darryl Kent
Mr Gay USA at Large 2005
Mister Liberty International Plus Emeritus
Mister Renaissance 2012

Denise Russell
Miss USofA at Large 1990
Miss Continental Plus 1992

Dey Jzah Opulent
Miss Texas Black America 2012

Freddy Prinze Charming
Mister Arizona USofA MI 2009
Mister Arizona USofA MI Emeritus
Mister Phoenix Gay Pride 2011

Gage Gatlyn
Master Male Illusionist Judge
Executive Producer / Promoter

Jay Santana
Judge-US of A,
FFI,
America,
and United States

Jayden Knight
Mr. Five Seasons FMI 2013

Jennifer Foxx
Miss Gay US of A 1996

Joey Jay/JR Heat
Miss National 2003

Kori Stevens
Miss Heart of Central Florida 2011
Co-Promoter, Florida All American Goddess

Mis Sadistic
Miss Key West Pageant 1999

Mykul Jay Valentine
Mr. Entertainer of the Year 2011

Natasha Richards
Miss Gay US of A 1996
Miss National 2003

Rico Taylor
Ms.Ter Pasco County 2012
Mr. Lake City Pride 2011
St. Pete Pride 2013

Sam Hare
USA Unlimited All divisions,
Judge, Promoter,
and Current National Contest Director
2011 – 2012

Stephanie Stuart
Miss Southeast Continental Elite 2010

Taina T. Norell
Miss Goddess 2012
Miss Tri County 2012

Tiffani Middlesexx
Miss Florida 1980

Tori Taylor
Miss Gay Universe At Large 2000

Ty Nolan
Mr Gay Universe 1997
Mr Greater Tampa 1982
Mr Gay USA At Large 2003
Mr Florida Leather 1997
Mr North Florida Drummer1996

Vinnie Marconi
Mister St. Pete Pride 2012
Mister Chill Chamber Emeritus 2011
Mister Gay Florida United States MI 2013

Vivika D'Angelo
Miss Gay Tucson America 2009

Limited commentary by
The Infamous Todd Kachinski Kottmeier, Creator and
Publisher of the DRAG411 books and DRAG411.com

> "I'm notorious for giving a bad interview. I'm an actor and I can't help but feel I'm boring when I'm on as myself."
> Rock Hudson

Chapter One

"Talk Easy"

Preparing for the "Personal Interview"

UNEDITED RESPONSES

AJ Menendez (<u>K</u>ING = K)

You should treat your interview for a competition like you would a job interview. It doesn't matter if you do it in male or female attire.

I personally do them in female attire, showing them the "Person" first and then later the Illusionist. When you are called in, NEVER sit until you are asked. Shake the hand of every judge in the room. EYE CONTACT is a MUST. Keep your answers short and to the point, don't babble. I made that mistake once... just once. Do not allow your nerves to show, be as relaxed as possible.

When the interview is over, stand up and once again shake the hand of every judge thanking them for the opportunity. Again, eye contact and smile. The biggest mistake you can make during an interview is lack of professionalism. You may not be walking into a "regular" job interview, but it IS an interview just the same.

Stephanie Stuart (<u>Q</u>ueen = Q)

Speak confidently. Always talk in a manner that makes you appear confident even when you aren't.

Amy Demilo (Q)

Know yourself, be yourself, know the system, the rules and regulations and the expectations of the titleholder. Different mistakes for different contestants. Mine is getting nervous...

Anastacia Dupree (Q)

What most contestants forget is this category is called INTERVIEW. Think of this as a job you are interviewing for. Systems want not only a talented person, but also someone who can be an administrator as well. Speak clearly; make eye contact with the person asking the question, dress professionally. ALWAYS were panty hose they don't care how good your legs look they want professionalism.

Anson Reign (K)

When I attend Personal Interview, I make it a point to shake hands and greet each judge when I enter, and then shake hands and thank each judge when I leave. It's a small detail, but it's always worked well for me. One of the biggest mistakes a contestant makes is being afraid of silence. When you are finished answering a question be finished. The judges will sit there quietly to make sure you are done speaking - give them that moment. Don't panic and try to fill the silence.

Natasha Richards (Q)

They are not themselves, they have to choose. If going to go in as a woman-don't leave with me thinking you're a man or vice versa.

Bob Taylor (Judge)

Inappropriate clothing, replying with "rehearsed" answers instead of "being themselves," and not being educated on the actual pageant system in which they are competing in.

Dana Douglas   (Q)

The biggest mistake you can make during interview is being shy. Don't be afraid to speak your mind and share your opinion. That's what the judges are looking for.

Breonna Tenae (Q)

To win personal Interview Be yourself, make eye contact, and hold a conversation with the judges. Never just answer questions. They are judging your ability to talk to anyone and self-confidence. Wow them with your real personality; fakes ones are always clocked.

Brittany T Moore (Q)

The biggest mistake is not being genuine and sincere. Judges can see that. Dress for success, look like a million dollars. Know the pageant system you are entering and why you would be their best representative

Coco Montrese (Q)

Many think that you tell the judges what "you think they want to hear" is how you win the personal interview. That is incorrect. Winning the male interview category out of fifty-two contestants, I can tell you, stay focused but honest, true to what you believe, and give your answer with the reason for your answer in a timely manner. Show the judges that you are stable, grounded, and confident in your answer. It is not always going be the answer they agree with, but delivery is very important.

Darryl Kent (Mr.)

Be yourself. It is key to allow judges to get to know you. No one in the world can answer questions about you better than you.

Denise Russell (Q)

You must be yourself! Look at the judges when answering questions. Be familiar with the Pageant system and know some of their history, such as former titleholders. Work on your vocabulary and don't use slang! Smile at the judges and show them you.

Jennifer Foxx   (Q)

Visually bring a clean physical product before the judge's panel. As a national titleholder and a judge of national pageantry I look for a contestant that carries on a conversation about him/herself without it sounding like an interrogation. In an interview, I want you to tell me who you are and why you are involved in this system.Be yourself, but project how you arrived in the seat (before me and the panel) with ease. We want to help you succeed, so relax and talk about yourself and your dreams. Do not digress or speak of other contests or contestants. Focus on you and your purpose.

Jay Santana (J)

Personal interview is the contestant's one opportunity to actually speak with the judges. When I interview contestants, I attempt to find out "what they will bring to the system other than the ability to entertain an audience." Are they professional? How will they duck and dodge drag drama. What is their work ethic and how will they assist in growing the system, etc. The biggest mistake I see during the interview portion of a pageant, is that contestant's spew out what they think we judges want to hear. These nearly cliché answers come off as fake, superficial, and quickly hurt them with the panel of judges.

Dey Jzah Opulent (Q)

Interview is about presentation. The way you present yourself in this category, is how you will be viewed until the end of the contest. The biggest mistake many contestants make, is creating a grand or "fake" a persona to appear to be something that they aren't. The advice "BE YOURSELF" really is the best way to win this category!

Freddy Prinze Charming (K)

Keeping answers short and to the point can be tricky for contestants. Many tend to ramble or waffle. Keeping the conversation relaxed and yet professional can also be an issue.

Gage Gatlyn (K)

To handle this category, just be you. It is essential that you can naturally coexist with fans and other entertainers!

Joey Jay/JR (K)

Have fun. "Interview" is a very professional atmosphere, but you need to be remembered. I tell all of my competitors, they need to pretend they are having a good conversation in a coffee shop. We are there to get to know *you* and we want to see you shine your brightest. An eloquent vocabulary is crucial, but you need to be you. Have a platform, a plan of action, and make them see that you are *hungry* for success. Think to yourself, "How can I stick out?" Have a sense of humor; make them laugh a little, but overall, have a blast in interview.

Jayden Knight (K)

When going into an interview, always dress as if you are going for a job interview. They want to see who you are outside of your impersonation persona. Shake each judge's hand entering and leaving. When you enter say "hello nice to meet you." Also a big mistake is using "uh and um." They will dock points for that.

Kori Stevens (Q)

BE YOURSELF. The purpose of this category is to give the judges the opportunity to get to know you. Be honest. Biggest mistake: Telling them what you think they WANT to hear.

Mis Sadistic (Q)

Some of the biggest mistakes that contestants make are not waiting for the interviewer to finish the question completely before starting to answer. This immediately sets a bad tone for the rest of your interview. Some other things are rambling or going off on a tangent. Don't loose focus and always be respectful. If a question catches you off guard, or catches the wrong way, don't react to it, stay calm. Repeat the question out loud giving yourself a chance to think before you answer. Repeating the question is always a good rule to follow. It shows you are paying attention. Remember to speak clearly and stay calm and relaxed, try not to talk to fast take your time and above all be genuine when speaking. If you are not, it comes across and everyone will see it. Be candid and truthful. Speak from your heart when you answer.

Mykul Jay Valentine (K)

Always come in looking your best. Remember, this is a JOB interview. Do your research on the system you are competing for. Know the formers and the history of the system. Try to make valid points without rambling. A lot of people try to always answer the questions first (if in group interview) and that is not necessary. Take time to sit and think before you answer. If the answer pops into your head right away, then please, feel free to answer first. If in a group interview, try to get to know the other competitors in your group so that way you can go in more relaxed. And always be polite and charming, remember your manners. And, if at all possible, avoid saying, "Uh..." and "Um..."

Sam Hare (Promoter)

The first step is always to study the system and their needs, as well as what they are looking for in a national titleholder. For example, Miss Continental may not have to sell preliminaries but Miss USA Unlimited would generally. For interview, study the category description, speak to the promoter and ask them questions about the system. Talk to the current reigning as well. Next, prepare for interview as if it is a job. Mock interviews are a huge help too because it helped to say the answers you have in your head. Ask some friends to interview you. Dress clean, nails clean, shoes clean; make eye contact with the judges. Shake hands, and have a plan for your year ready to layout. The biggest mistakes I have seen over and over are the contestant being unprepared, unprofessional, and not understanding the system they are competing in at the time. The majorities of contestants do not have a plan of action and/or do not read the category description and sub-category.

Rico Taylor (K)

The biggest mistakes is going in too cocky or uncomfortable. Be yourself, be respectful, shake the judge's hand, introduce yourself and be very comfy with yourself and who you are it will go a long way.

Vinnie Marconi (K)

Be Sincere & Honest in your answer. Take a moment to think about what you will say. "Umm" is not acceptable! Do not say anything until you think of something worthwhile for the judges to hear. Keep your answer simple and on point. Remember, it's an interview. Treat it like any other job interview. Dress for success!

Taina T. Norell (Q)

Don't bite your nails, shake a leg, or make gestures with your hands while speaking. Ask if you can have a sit when you enter the room. Ig you don't ask first, you come across being rude!

Tiffani Middlesexx (Q)

Interview can be a very tricky part of any pageant. Dress appropriately. Wear something casual, but clean and sophisticated. Don't be nervous. Don't take all day to answer. Get to the point!

Tori Taylor (Q)

Be yourself, the biggest mistake is trying to tell the judges what you think they want to hear. You'd be surprised. They really just want to know the truth.

Ty Nolan (M)

Know the system and their history. Dress appropriately in suitable business attire. Be courteous and confident but not cocky. Do not sit until you are asked. Try not to use a lot of hand motions to talk. Do not take over the interview by over-answer.

Vivika D'Angelo (Q)

Interview for me is a challenge cause i speak about past present and future but i fail due to which i get nervous and not speak properly others i have heard either they fig-it or wonder off into outer space or don't talk enough so judges have to ask questions outside of the box.

**"When I stand before God at the end of my life,
I would hope that I would not have a single bit of talent left, and
could say, 'I used everything you gave me."**
Erma Bombeck

Chapter Two

"Second Verse,
Same As The First"

Winning Talent

UNEDITED RESPONSES
❀ ❀ ❀

Amy Demilo

To win "talent," keep it clean and entertaining. The biggest mistake is to over produce~

Anastacia Dupree

Talent should be easy right? Think again. A winning talent is not about how much you dance or how many dancers you have. Remember they will not travel with you if you win. Your talent should tell a story from start to finish. I have seen a lot of great ideas executed wrong and they flat-lined in the middle. Once you loose the judges attention it is very hard to get it back.

Anson Reign

Bring something more than a "bar number." If it's something I can see any Saturday night at the local drag club, it is not an appropriate pageant Talent number. One of the biggest mistakes contestants make in this category is being sloppy - the judges would rather see three people dancing together in synch than 15 people not well prepared and flopping all over the stage.

Vivika D'Angelo

Talent is a high scored category many fail if back up dancers are not on point or giving no energy.

Brittany T Moore

Biggest mistake is not rehearsing enough. Talents need to tell a story beginning middle to end.

Joey Jay/JR Heat

Talent is the in the hands of five to seven opinions. That's it. Your job as an entertainer is to, oh wait... entertain. Make them eager to see what happens next. Too many times judges get bored because mixes or numbers drag on and on. The most common error is the "when in doubt, take the wig off" strategy. Don't do it. It's not impressive, and it degrades you. Like interview, have a blast with "Talent," have a storyline, an introduction, bridge, climax, second climax (to really keep them on their toes) and a conclusion. That doesn't mean one song beginning to end.

AJ Menendez

It's been my own experience that when your talent number sends an important message, it's a winner. Not all entertainers do the same, it's to each entertainers discretion. Your talent number should not be any more than 6 to 7 minutes long, make sure you check with the promoters if you are unsure. Make sure your costuming is on point, zippers zipped, lint removed, no strings hanging, fits correctly etc.....Work the crowd to show your stage presence, but your main focus should be on the judges. Eye contact is a must once again. Unless told otherwise, never step off the stage during a pageant. You cannot accept tips. Again, if your nerves are blindsiding you, put them in check until afterward. Choreography should be on point and your lip sync should be flawless. Never hit the stage if you don't know the words as if you wrote the song.

Jennifer Foxx

Preparation meets opportunity equals success. Period. Do not overestimate your talents. Orchestrate a comprehensive talent piece that you are comfortable with executing and carry it through to the best of your ability. Do not be overly ambitious.

Jay Santana

With the talent portion of the pageant, I fully expect to be entertained at the highest level. I am always the most impressed with a contestant who performs live versus simply lip-syncing a song. The mere fact that a contestant is willing to take the risk of performing live is a plus. The biggest mistakes made in the talent portion of the pageant include being off as they lip sync, dancers out off rhythm, and hair or wardrobe malfunctions.

Mykul Jay Valentine

This category is exactly what it says, "Talent." What talents do you possess? How can you put your talent on stage impress the judges. A big mistake includes productions where your own dancers (and everyone else in the number) upstage you. You always want to be the center of attention. If you do a solo act, that's fine, there is nothing wrong with a solo talent. Sometimes people think they can't win because they don't have a big production. But that is not always the case. A solo talent can be just as good as any other talent.

Jayden Knight

When doing a talent you want a production number. You want something with a lot of energy or a lot of emotion. Judges love song mixes and dancing. A big mistake is if the costumes are not secure and pieces fly off; they will dock you. Also they will dock points for not knowing words and not enough eccentricity. Make sure you show a lot of emotion if you do a slow song make.

Dey Jzah Opulent

Talent like interview is about presentation as well. How you present your talent. I always say to follow the three C's! Concept, Costuming, and Conditioning. A perfect talent almost needs to tell a story. Most judges are intrigued when they know what's going on and if the talent has a cohesive beginning to finale. You don't want the judges to be puzzled about happening on stage. Your points will suffer greatly if they confused. Make sure that while you're telling this story that your costumes are not only helping with that but that they look great. I've seen many talents where the actual talent was great, but the costumes where so shabby and they affected the outcome score. Conditioning plays a heavy part in your talent. DO NOT DO ANYTHING YOU AREN'T FIT TO DO! Contestants create a big mistake by trying to over exert themselves beyond their capabilities. Perform the act you rehearsed and fit to do. There is nothing worse than seeing an incomplete talent displayed because the entertainer is winded.

Coco Montrese

Talent should always showcase what you do best and should always have a meaning or a story (reasoning) behind it. Beginning. Middle. End. A big mistake is picking a song with a great beat and they just dance. For example if you're going do "Last Dance" by Donna Summer, the judges have to feel like it's really your last dance, know the works you are "singing" about . Don't pick a talent just because everyone else is doing it, make it your own!

Dana Douglas

Never let your production or dancers out shine you. Whatever you do "must feature you" at all times!

Darryl Kent

Don't keep it too safe. A lot of entertainers live by the motto, "If it ain't broke don't fix it." Success with a certain talent does not mean that it is the only talent you could do to score well. Be creative, unique, take chances.

Bob Taylor

Winning this category is subjective. Entertainment is different for everyone, including the judges selected. Biggest mistake is missing the details. REHEARSE your talent in a club in front of an audience BEFORE competing.

Denise Russell

This the one category I always won! To me it is the most important category. Club owners won't book you based on your interview skills or because you wore a pretty gown, they book you for your TALENT! The best talent numbers always tell a story. There needs to be a beginning, middle and ending. Don't be fooled into thinking that comedy does not win pageants. I won two national titles performing comedy. In a Talent competition, you have seven minutes, so use your time wisely. Do what you do best. Too often queens fail to play to their strengths. If you are not a great dancer, DON"T dance. The one thing above all else, if you lip sync, you should KNOW the words! I need to believe you are singing!

Freddy Prinze Charming

Talent should be something the audience and judges understand. The best talents I've seen have a point or a story easily understood and relatable. Don't come to a pageant with something akin to a bar number, where there has been very little extra effort put forth.

Gage Gatlyn

It should be comprised of great stage presence and choreography; he should be convincing and have great costuming. The whole package is judged. Biggest mistake: Underestimating your competition or bringing your average "Bar number."

Ty Nolan

Be prepared, know your material. You must be entertaining and emotional whether it is comedy, music, or a theatrical production. Choose appropriate costumes and props, if allowed. Be original and again, be prepared! Biggest mistakes: lip syncing, dancers or props distracting due to the number on stage (or they are not in unison).

Kori Stevens

Stay true to yourself. Feel comfortable doing your routine and keep it clean.

Mis Sadistic

I feel some of the biggest mistakes made by contestants in the talent category are not fully being rehearsed and/or prepared. You must know your talent number inside and out. Keep in mind, if there is a mishap, not to stop or let it throw you off. You are the only one who would know, in most cases. In the event something does go wrong (example: if you were to fall on stage) keep on going, stay in character and by all means finish with grace and dignity. Try to remember not every performance will be perfect, but how you handle it must be.

Natasha Richard

Tell a story. You must have a beginning, middle and an end. It should be a ride on a roller coaster that makes the judge want to ride again.

Rico Taylor

Biggest mistake for talent; not knowing the words or routine you made for yourself. Don't wear regular street clothes; it will get your score hammered low!

Sam Hare

Step one: be entertaining! Talent needs to be thought out, again read the category description several times to start. You must be entertaining, and since it is a competition, if you want to win you need to be the most entertaining. It is also vital to read the sub-categories and the criteria for scoring. The contestant does not always have to have twenty people behind them. The more people in the talent, the most likely to make a mistake.

Contestants should always remain the star of the talent, back-up dancers need to know their place and be equally matched. Costumes should be cleaned, wrinkle free, and not have strings. The last step is practice, practice, practice. Then practice more.

The biggest mistake made by contestants is not starting to prepare soon enough to plan the talent, have costumes, talent mix, and practice. Contestants should have everything for a national pageant complete and ready no less than two weeks prior to registration. Talent should be put together and ready a month or more to give time to practice. You get out of it what you put into it when it comes to talent!

Tiffani Middlesexx

Know your music. Try and perform a dance production. They seem to go over better with judges and audiences

Stephanie Stuart

Don't over think talent. If you take on too much and it becomes a mess at pageant time.

Tori Taylor

Tell a story, make sure you have a beginning middle and ending. Nothing should be left out, except the longing for more…

Taina T. Norell

REHEARSE. When you don't rehearse, it will show the day off the pageant. Take (at least) a month prior to your event to get the dancers, people, and the props you will use on stage. Rehearsing is the key to a winning talent!

Breonna Tenae

Talent should be practiced to perfection. Never step in front of judges doing something you are uncomfortable with. Make eye contact with the judges. Make them want to jump out of their seats and join you on stage. Entertain. Entertain. Entertain. This is where you stop being yourself, become your character, and create a great show!

No matter how loud the crowd may scream, keep your focus on the judges as they are the ones you are trying to win over!

It should be the same rule for your backup dancers. Make sure they are all on cue and point, yet at all times have fun! Don't be so serious that your presence looses its luster.

Vinnie Marconi

Winning Talent is often the most difficult category to win.

If you can't RECITE your words without music, then you don't know it well enough. WORK, WORK, WORK!

**"It usually takes me more than three weeks
to prepare a good impromptu speech."**
Mark Twain

Chapter Three

"Grateful Thought and Contemplation" Winning the On Stage Question"

UNEDITED RESPONSES

Mykul Jay Valentine

On stage question and answer is tough, because you are put on the spot. Everyone is paying attention to you. You have to come up with a winning answer to a random question right then and there. It's hard. Just remember to take a deep breath, calm yourself down, and answer the question. Many people ramble on trying to get their point across. They never actually answer the question, so they lose the category.

Vinnie Marconi

"Umm," should NEVER pass your lips! The judges want to know how you handle situations should you wear the crown. Be honest and sincere. I try to use personal experience to bring it home.

Ty Nolan

Be confident, aware of local events, and know your platform. If you are asked about it, think about your question in a timely manner. Give precise, to the point answers. Biggest mistakes: running around the question, not being specific, or answering the question.

Natasha Richards

Q and A is one of the most valuable. Always say the first thing that comes to your mind. People want to hear what is in your heart, what it feels like then and there. Thinking too much is your enemy. Say it as you feel it.

Tori Taylor

Think before you speak. Be clear, quick, and do not drag it out.

Taina T Norell

Take a deep breath, don't over think it, don't lie, and just be as quick and honest as possible (but keep it within two minutes).

Stephanie Stuart

Speak from the heart. Be direct! Don't take too long, keep it short and sweet. End it with laughter when possible! Don't use "um and hums" never, ever!

DeyJzah Opulent Mirage

Speak clearly, think about the question before you answer, and don't be afraid to pause to collect your thoughts. The goal is to answer the question, not on how fast you can answer it. The biggest mistake contestants make in this category is not pacing their words or allowing a moment to gather their thoughts.

Bob Taylor

Your answer should always come from your heart, not a rehearsed or answer you think the judges want to hear. Be who YOU are and answer honestly. Biggest mistake is losing your concentration when hearing the question.

Anson Reign

Begin by thanking the judges and greeting the audience. Keep your answer brief, succinct and to the point – with no more than one or two complete sentences. Don't ramble!

Sam Hare

The main thing to remember for any on-stage question is to relax, take a deep breath, and take your time. I have judged many on-stage question competitions and never took points away because the contestant paused thirty to forty seconds to think. Never! This is another category where you can have friends in the industry put ten questions in envelopes, stand up in front of them, pick each question, and answer it out loud. This helps contestants tremendously.The biggest mistake I have seen at almost every pageant is "contestants trying to over-answer, over-elaborate, talk too long, and in circles. The best advice is to keep your answers short and to the point. Listen to the question, repeat it to yourself, think of a couple of key words or points you want to make, make them, and stop. Less is most often more in the case of on-stage question.

Jayden Knight

Always make sure to thank the judges, venue and fans. Big mistakes include speaking too fast or stumbling over your words. Remember to speak slowly and clearly.

Amy DeMilo

Speak from the heart. A mistake is to ramble.

Mis Sadistic

When it comes to having success with random on stage questions, you should always repeat the question asked before you begin your answer. Always answer clearly and articulately with your voice up so the last person in the back row can hear you with ease. Stay on topic and do not go off on a tangent.

Kori Stevens

Keep it clear and concise. No need to tell long drawn out stories. Don't be afraid to take a moment to think.

Joey Jay/JR Heat

Many contestants jump right in because they feel they need to speak right away so they "know their stuff." Nobody wants a know-it-all as a title holder. Take your time. Take a few deep breaths while you think of a good answer, allowing yourself to organize your thoughts, and then proceed. Lastly, people should be able to relate to your answer. Make it personal... you want to capture these judges.

Jennifer Foxx

On Stage question is ONLY YOUR OPINION. There is no wrong or right answer. Do not try to come up with something to make the audience applaud. The audience is not judging you, you are being judged by the panel. Remove yourself from the moment. Think of how you would best answer this question, if you were with your best friend at home eating pizza asked it. It is your unique answer. Breath, compute, and then you can answer with respect and humility.

Freddy Prinze Charming

I've seen many contestants simply fail to answer the question. They ramble on far too long. I've also seen contestants manage to insult previous title holders in their answers.

Jay Santana

The on stage question is the contestant's last opportunity to make an impression on the panel of judges and audience. I listen to see if the contestant actually addresses the heart of the question or if they, like politicians, dance around the question and really say nothing. It is imperative that the question asked is addressed, period. The single biggest mistake off the "on stage question" portion of the pageant is that the contestant fails to address the question asked.

Coco Montrese

The biggest mistake in Q & A is long answers. Literally, just answer what is asked. It leaves room for less error

Gage Gatlyn

No props and no back up dancers are allowed here. Stage presence and costuming plays a big part in this category. You must be able to "hold your own" and entertain the audience all by yourself. The biggest mistake here is not believing your words or standing in one place. You have to find a way to keep your audience's attention without all the 'static'.

Denise Russell

Practice at home! Have friends ask you questions. This will make it easier for you on pageant night. This category has brought down many queens. Take your time answering and answer only the question that you were asked.

Darryl Kent

The biggest mistake I see contestants make is not listening closely to the question. They focus on a keyword they hear and often tune out the rest. It is disastrous when the entire meaning of the question is misinterpreted due to not listening.

Anastacia Dupree

REPEAT THE QUESTION. Many don't do this. Speak clearly and keep it short; you should be on and off.

Brittany T Moore

Biggest mistake is not answering the question. Listen to the question and answer it completely.

Dana Douglas

Don't over think it. Just answer the question completely. They usually follow a question by asking "Why?" Don't get so carried away with the first part that you forget the "Why?" Keep it short and sweet.

Vivika D'Angelo

Most answer it with a longer answer than needed or answer the with nothing to do with the original question.

Breonna Tenae

On stage question is your time to speak in public. Always address the judges, say your name, repeat your questions, and answer it. Period. Nothing special here, just answer the question given, do not elaborate, be confident, and speak up!

AJ Menendez

This is my least favorite category!
Do not enter this category wearing your costume, wear your crowing outfit. Display professionalism. Don't think about your answer too long, be confident, and to the point.

"Everyone said, loud enough for the others to hear:
"Look at the Emperor's new clothes. They're beautiful!"
"What a marvelous train!"
"And the colors. The colors of that beautiful fabric!
I have never seen anything like it in my life!""
from The Emperor's New Clothes
by Hans Christian Anderson

Chapter Four

"Are the fancy clothes you see in the mirror, the same wardrobe others see on you too?"

Eveningwear

By now you realize, reaching for the crown has the same path for Kings, Queens, Misters, Pageants, Contests, and Shows. Performers thinking the path is vastly different are often those that do not understand, winning has nothing to do with your sexual orientation, but your character, morals, drive, and confidence.

UNEDITED RESPONSES

Bob Taylor

Each pageant system has a "sort of style" preferred in their system. STUDY THE SYSTEM Also, gown fit, color, design... all very important. Do not wear appropriate hair and accessories.

Freddy Prinze Charming

There is a fine line between creative eveningwear and a costume. Not enough creativity and you basically just have a suit or a dress. But being too over the top can also be an issue. It should still be wearable and realistic, without being too costumy.

Tiffani Middlesexx

Biggest mistake is queen wearing too tight gowns.

Amy DeMilo

The fit and how you wear it is everything; too long, too short, too big, too small, so many mistakes.

DeyJzah Opulent Mirage

Winning this category is about knowing who you are. Know your personal style and how to make yourself look great. Be aware of your physical attributes you want displayed in this category, it will get you far. Keep in mind, usually when being judge for gown its not just the gown being judged. Shoes, hair, accessories and makeup all play a big part in your over all score.

Brittany T Moore

You need a perfect fit. The color needs to go with your skin. Everything matters, the shoes, jewelry, hair, and makeup.

Denise Russell

The only advice I can give is make sure your gown is in GREAT shape and that it fits your body properly! Don't over do the jewelry!

Sam Hare

Read the category description because most are slightly different. Find a gown or formalwear that fits the description, and make sure you have hair and jewelry that do not overpower but compliment the outfit. Always make sure it fits (this is one of the biggest mistakes). If you borrow an outfit, have it fitted to you, even if it is temporarily stitched. Invest in something of your own that someone fit onto your body. Another big step is having a dresser! Pay someone if needed, but have a dresser that can keep you focused. Make sure you look ready for the spotlight. Please keep a flashlight with you to shine backstage to catch strings and other issues. The spotlight is blinding. It shows everything you won't see, so a flashlight is a big help. The biggest mistakes I find are the fit issues with garments. Biggest mistakes include borrowing something last minute, not having your own dresser, and looking messy. Make sure you are smiling on stage and ready to face your judges.

Vinnie Marconi

Accentuate the positive, be it broad shoulders or long legs. If the suit isn't a PERFECT fit, have it tailored. The accessories can make or break the most expensive suit. A splash of color with matching cufflinks and shoes, or a matching feather in the cap will bring a TOTAL look to the table. ATTITUDE is KEY! Be confident and suave in your modeling and don't "cheese" a smile, the judges see that! They want YOUR personality to shine through in EVERY aspect of the competition; don't forget to show personality here, too.

Coco Montrese

Wear what fits and is comfortable to you the individual, that's very important, biggest mistake is picking a gown based on its beauty and not being able to walk in it.

Anson Reign

No matter how pretty or shiny your outfit is, if it doesn't fit you perfectly, you will not score well in this category. That's my advice, as well as one of the biggest mistakes contestants make in the Eveningwear category.

Vivika D'Angelo

Having a gown too short or not fit right is a big issue plus making sure that the color and cut of the gown is proper for your look.

Darryl Kent

Find something that fits you both physically and personality wise. If you are comfortable in your clothing, your modeling will show it, while if you try to wear something cumbersome or couture without the attributes to carry it off, it could be a problem for you.

Anastacia Dupree

The fit is the most important and how you model the gown. If you don't feel comfortable, the judge can tell. You spend lots of money on a gown. It is up to you to sell this gown to the judges. Gowns from your local department store will not work; have something made to fit your body.

Stephanie Stuart

Make sure your gown fits correctly. Accessories are a necessity along with clean smooth hair. Your gown needs to be a fantasy; a gown no woman can wear but every woman wants to wear!

Tori Taylor

Take your time, do not show off the gown... wear the gown. Do not let it wear you.

Rico Taylor

Make sure your eveningwear is properly fitted and works for you and your style. Make sure you are comfy walking in it and showing your personality for the Male Illusionist (MI) judges. Make it a well-tailored suit or something rather formal or creative. Mistakes often include mismatched colors, black suits, not buying the whole thing (only pieces), and it not fitting. Have the right song and practice your walk.

Breonna Tenae

Eveningwear is just that, model your eveningwear. Present it as if you were stepping out to the Grammy's and doing a red carpet. Confidence, confidence, confidence. Be graceful at all times, smile, and flirt with your judges panel. Don't be afraid of getting too close. Remember your points and turns. Do them with style and elegance, and most of all… smile! Show them the inner beauty, as well as out. Keep your movements soft and smooth. Show the whole package; gown accessories and makeup. Learn posing and facial expressions in the mirror. Showcase your makeup application and skill. Hair should be up or away from your face. Never look down and always keep eye contact!

Taina T Norell

I see many short dresses on contestants; the fit says it all. I don't care what dress you decide to wear, it has to fit your body and it has to touch the floor when you're wearing your heels. Otherwise, you're going to loose the easiest category in the pageant (which is my favorite category of the competition).

Freddy Prinze Charming

There is a fine line between creative eveningwear and a costume. Without enough creativity and you basically just have a suit or a dress. Being too "over the top" can also become an issue. It should still be wearable and realistic, without being too costumey.

Jay Santana

The eveningwear portion of the pageant is where I expect perfection. The hair must be formal appropriate; make up must be flawless; accessories must ACCENT the eveningwear, NOT overpower it. Their pantyhose must not be run; no lint on suits/tuxes, no scuffs on shoes. The biggest mistake I is not being comfortable modeling their eveningwear.

Mykul Jay Valentine

You want to make sure you have an outfit that fits you perfectly. You will want to have it tailored to fit you. Make sure the style and color of the suit is flattering to your body and skin tone. Many people make the mistake to get a suit too big or short on the arms or legs. The arm should hit just right above the thumb knuckle and the leg should hit right about where the sole of the shoe and the sock meet. Also, think "head to toe." Do the shoes match? A lot of people don't think in "Creative Formal Wear" to rhinestone their shoes., but a little goes a long way. A rhinestone shoe might give it the extra little pop you need to win this catagory.

Dana Douglas

Evening gown must fit perfectly. Length must touch the top of you toes in front and to the floor in the back. Must fit with out bunching or pulling and always choose a color that compliments you. Don't spend a fortune on a dress and not practice walking in it. If you can't walk in it, you've wasted a fortune.

AJ Menendez

If it's just regular formal wear, make sure your suit / tux is fitted to your specifications! Your pants leg should go up to the top of the sole of your shoe, your jacket sleeve should go down to the top of your thumb knuckle. Your shirt should fit your neck size exactly. Your outfit should be freshly pressed and all lint removed. When choosing your Formal Wear music, make sure it's a song you can glide across the stage to and model. Again, don't let your nerves show. Always use a T walk* when modeling. Look at each judge and smile. Show your personality; own the stage. Biggest mistake: wrinkles. Make sure you have none and your suit fits to a tee.

Jennifer Foxx

Evening gown is about comfort ability in one's own skin. Bigger is not always better. It is how you look in your garment of choice and how you sell your beauty in this garment. HOWEVER you must be clean on all accounts. ALWAYS buy new shoes, keep jewelry to a minimum. MOST OF ALL... stop replicating the looks of other performers. Everyone does not have to wear an up-do, necklace, and big matching ring. Be yourself; it will ultimately service you.

Mis Sadistic

When it comes to eveningwear, I feel some of the biggest mistakes are in picking the wrong outfit. To give an example: A dress not fitting well. You must keep in mind how you are built, your body type. What you wear should fit you like a second skin and move with you effortlessly. In other words, your shape and size should be taken into consideration when buying your eveningwear. A dress fitting the contestant right, should not limit mobility. If a dress has too much fabric, like a much exaggerated train or over sized ball gown, a contestant cannot gracefully walk across the stage with a seamless presentation. Dress accordingly; eveningwear should be just that. A contestant should not have on a cocktail dress or bar wear; this is your time to show your elegance. Walk slowly and take your time, own the stage and the runway.

Kori Stevens

Make sure the ensemble is in good condition and fits well, especially in length. Make sure your hair is neatly pulled together (whether up or down), and you move at a comfortable pace for you.

Jayden Knight

When modeling eveningwear, you want to make sure you walk all of the stage until they announce your name and contestant number. Always remember to have a couple different poses and walk by the judges, and always smile. A big mistake is leaving the stage too soon.
Models enter the runway from one side of the "T" and exit on the other.

Joey Jay/JR Heat

If I have seen it already, my interest is gone. Originality and how it fits is the best answer for any type of eveningwear. Give it a few test tries before you walk on the stage with it. Make sure it moves and shows off "your body," nobody else's.

Natasha Richards

Start with something you love, fit and feel comfortable wearing. Your movements are imperative. You must be comfortable to make the next girl feel uncomfortable. You are there to win, and once again, tell your story.

Ty Nolan

Make sure eveningwear fits, is fashionable and flawless. Know your system to assist in what type of eveningwear is required. Biggest mistakes: fit and flaws.

Jay Santana

The eveningwear portion of the pageant is where I expect perfection!! The hair must be formal appropriate; make up must be flawless; accessories must ACCENT the eveningwear NOT overpower it. Your hose must not run; no lint on suits/tuxes, and no scuffs on shoes!

"I don't design clothes,
I design dreams."
Ralph Lauren

Chapter Five

"Accentuate your Creativity"

In the Creativity category

UNEDITED RESPONSES

❀ ❀ ❀

Bob Taylor

Creativity is subjective.

Amy DeMilo

Creative is the key word. Costume, music selection, makeup, all factors on winning.. Mistake is wearing a sat night show costume...

DeyJzah Opulent Mirage

The category is creative costume... use your imagination.. If you believe it and put the work into it...it should be magical!

Brittany T Moore

Be creative. Think outside the box and study the judges.

Freddy Prinze Charming

Your costume should work with the theme or performance. Ideally, it should flow as a unit without being full of disjointed pieces and accessories.

AJ Menendez

Bring your own creativity to your outfit with painting, stoning, sequence...whatever. They are looking to see how creative you are in addition to the fit of your outfit.

Vinnie Marconi

I've been told, and so far it's worked, that there is no such thing as too much when it comes to this category. Think outside your comfort zone and PILE IT ON. Go the extra ten miles; do your homework, research the theme, go 3 pages into the search before you start paying attention. This is what the judges won't expect, than take it over the top!

Coco Montrese

This category is just what it says creative, be over the top and make it functional, biggest mistake, costumes that are difficult to model.

Anson Reign

Advice: go big or go home. A mistake is making too much of a statement, which can get in the way of the creativity the judges seek.

Vivika D'Angelo

Costume not representing what you are telling in a song.

Sam Hare

The first step again is read the category description and the criteria involved. Please ahead, figure out what looks good onstage and what you're able to walk in onstage. Make sure it makes sense and is complete. The biggest mistakes that I see are contestants putting together homemade costumes and they are not ready for the spotlight of the stage. Beads and pieces falling off, glue or makeup or dirt on the costume.

Anastacia Dupree

This is my favorite category. You get to go wild and let the creativity juices flow. The biggest mistake I have seen is people copying someone else and changing it just a little. Remember it is Creative Costume, so be original.

Stephanie Stuart

Go way out of the box let your mind run free and create from there!

Rico Taylor

Creative costume is what the judges want to see how you use your imagination and skills as a professional and see how well you stick in the theme it's always fun wing creative and stepping outside the box but if you step out make sure you match the theme or do go over board.

Breonna Tenae

Creative costume is the most fun because you get to show your creativity show case your creative fashion in a way that you personality blends with the costume be playful and act out any elements that help paint the mental picture of your creation.

Darryl Kent

Remember that creativity is the key. Creativity is not copying someone else's old idea, it is not revamping someone's old idea, and it is presenting your idea tastefully and creatively.

Tori Taylor

Think outside the box.

Tiffani Middlesexx

Be creative use your imagination.

Natasha Richards

The biggest mistake I've seen in Creative Costume is when the creative costume is not your own. You must rack your brain to be creative, on your own. Then bring it to life.

Taina T Norell

Do a research on the theme and stay focus on that!

Jay Santana

Creative costume needs to be a reflection of the contestant as well as keep in touch with the theme of the pageant. The contestant must look within to find their creative voice and merge their creativity with the theme they have been handed. The biggest mistake I see is a contestant buys something off the shelf and parades across the stage thinking it is creative.

Mykul Jay Valentine

Creative costume is exactly what it says, a COSTUME. A lot of time people will make costumes that completely cover those head to toe. Which, looks cool, but that doesn't work in a pageant. My advice on this category is, "Think outside the box." Do your research, see what hasn't been done.

Dana Douglas

Originality! Something they've never seen before, verse's a poor copy of something we've all seen a million times.

Jennifer Foxx

Hire the people that are best in this area and invest heavily. Do NOT replicate concepts that have succeeded in former pageants. As a judge I discount the efforts that are not genuine.

Kori Stevens

Creativity is the key! Try not to replicate something that another entertainer has done. Use original ideas, and make sure they are executed properly.

Jayden Knight

Always be eccentric. Big mistake is holding back on your creativity.

Joey Jay

Once again, originality.

Mis Sadistic

The biggest mistakes are picking an outfit with limited visibility or restricted movement; this will impede your presentation. Having a hot costume and falling down in it because your visibility is so limited can make for a huge mistake. A contestant should not have a headdress that is so large they cannot handle it. They should not have to hold it up with one hand to help support it because it is falling off to one side or the other. A costume should not restrict your movements. If it is too big and you cannot comfortably walk or move your arms around, you're not showing your full potential. You want a judge to be taken back in a good way to have them wanting more, wow them. The costume should fit and flow with you. Again your costume should be unique, yet fit like a second skin and if there is theme, stick to the theme. The creative costume should fit the contestant's entire package.

Ty Nolan

Creativity, creativity, creativity... enough said! Appropriate to theme of contest, if applicable. Biggest mistakes: Originality.

Gage Gatlyn

The biggest mistake: Jeans and T-Shirt.... This is the contestant's chance to SHINE! Show us what you got.... Show us your creativity... Show the world there is so much more to a Drag King than a three dollar mustache and a pair of jeans.

**"Great dancers are not great because of their technique;
they are great because of their passion."**
Martha Graham

Chapter Six

Steps to successfully prepare to win with "Props and Backup Dancers"

UNEDITED RESPONSES

Bob Taylor

Be careful when hiring dancers. Are they dependable? Do they upstage you when performing? Do they drink or other? If you are paying them then they MUST be treated respectfully as employees. Props... are they needed. Are they a distraction? REHEARSE using them as much as possible."

Amy DeMilo

Practice, practice, and practice with props and dancers. Videoing rehearsals are always a good idea.... Mistakes include too many dancers and overwhelming props...

Coco Montrese

Biggest mistakes with props and back up dancers are when you have to many of either, if not well put together any of these could be a major distraction.

DeyJzah Opulent Mirage

Props are a big part of production presentation...they are extra credits toward presenting a talent and if are done right, help with telling your story and are assembled correctly, you can't go wrong with using them. Same with backup dancers, however make sure that neither your props nor your dancers upstage you. They are there as helpers to tell your story, you are the star and should always appear as such throughout the duration of your presentation.

Brittany Moore

Pick people that are on your team to win and make sure you know the stage you while performing and to make sure your talent fits.

Vinnie Marconi

I use a myriad of props and back-ups in a regular performance. For pageants, however, I give myself 6 weeks to 2 months to work with them. My props are either practical, functional, or drive home a point but they ALWAYS have to help tell a story. I have fittings and get costumes made even before the first practice. Choreography (not my forte) is ALWAYS trial and error until you find what works for the group as a whole and spotlights YOU. Then I do a private YouTube video of EACH person's part so when we CAN all come together again, they've had something to practice with. As far as the props, DON'T be chintzy. It will cost you in the end.

Denise Russell

Remember, YOU are to be the center of attention in you talent number! If you use props, make sure they are well made! No judge wants to see props that look like a high school production of Fiddler on the Roof" If you choose to use back-up dancers, don't let them out dance you. and don't let them steal the spotlight! YOU are the STAR of the production!"

Anson Reign

Make it special and memorable. Don't build a set specifically for the sole purpose of having a set - make sure to incorporate it, and that it makes sense with your number. One of the biggest mistakes a contestant can make is allowing themselves to be upstaged by their dancers (or their set.) No matter what YOU need to be the focus of your number.

Vivika D'Angelo

Backup dancers not on point if one misses a step it all does down hill from their props with any mechanical devices that don't work are also an issue.

Sam Hare

Props - make sure the prop is needed and necessary. Then make sure it can be set-up in the time limit and it is complete. Practice prop set-up time. Back-up dancers need to be dressed appropriately, even down to the same shoes, and evenly matched. Tell them you are the star and they are not competing with you or each other. They should not be chewing gum unless it is in the role, and they should not be lip syncing unless they are supposed to be in a lip syncing part. The biggest mistakes for back-up dancers is lack of practice, outfits that look cheap or unmatched on-stage, and dancers that are out dancing each other on-stage.

Anastacia Dupree

Your props should look professional not something that is hot glued together or falls over. Dancers what can i say make sure they know the dance....

Stephanie Stuart

The biggest mistake with dancers is they can out dance you! You must be as strong of a dancer as they are. And props tend to fall down make them sturdy!

Rico Taylor

Make sure your props or back ups are on the same page as you (routine wise or anything such as costume). You don't want back ups upstaging you or out dancing you. It makes you look bad. Props should be well made and fit the song.

Breonna Tenae

Do practice runs to get your timing right and make sure props are reinforced and sturdy make sure every one knows the stage and points to be so when the music starts every one is focused on the performance and not wondering or worried about props Practice run-throughs with your stage hands and dancers to make sure set up is just as on point as the actually talent. Judges don't score this behind the scenes part of a talent but trust me they are watching and it shows up in the over all talent score.

Darryl Kent

The biggest issue I find is props that look cheap or add very little to the production value. If they don't look authentic or well done, leave them out. As far as dancers go, don't hire professionals who clearly out dance you if you are not a trained dancer or can keep up with them. Also, don't force people into your talent just for the sake of it being a production if it doesn't make sense in the overall presentation of your talent.

Tori Taylor

Too many back up dancers is a good way to lose points, they are you.

Jay Santana

Props and backup dancers should, like jewelry, be an accent to the performance. Biggest mistake made in this area by allowing the props or dancers to outshine the contestant.

Taina T Norell

Rehearsing seems to be the biggest mistakes some contestants make. It doesn't matter if you have done the number a million times. Practice makes perfect" if the pageant is within a month practice with your dancers every week at least for four hours. If you don't know your talent while you're showering eating or while your going to bed, most likely your going to lose this category!

Mykul Jay Valentine

If you are going to use a prop, make sure it's not in the way, not tacky, and moves on and off quickly. Don't just throw something together. Take your time to make it nice. Backup dancers are always a great idea. Just be careful with them. You never want them to upstage you, always use them to accentuate yourself. Make sure you practice, practice, practice! Timing always seems to be an issue when it comes to backup dancers. And you really don't need to fill up the stage with as many dancers as you can. If just one messes up, then they could lose the whole thing for you. Only use people you know are good, and trust.

Dana Douglas

If at all possible, it more cost effective to hire professional dancers in the city where the pageant is being held. You save in hotel and airfare for one, and you don't have to worry about personal drama that always seems to happen when using friends. Pros are there to do their job. That is all...

Jennifer Foxx

Never have a back-up group that is shorter than you in stature, it makes you look manly. Never dance with real women, unless you are as convincing and beautiful as your team. Never let your presentation overwhelm you as an individual. Do not get lost in your number.

Mis Sadistic

I feel the biggest mistakes when it comes to props are not having them well constructed. Remember they have to hold up in transit. Things get bounced around going to and from a pageant venue. Anything you plan on using in your performance should hold up so you don't have a prop break in the middle of a performance or even worse not have it because it is unusable before you even begin. This really is a two part question for me. When it comes to back up dancers above all reliability and knowing there routine is everything. There is nothing worse than on pageant night if a dancer or dancers don't show. You need to have trustworthy people working with you. Practice makes perfect, you don't want your backup dancer to make a mistake in choreography. Even if you are perfect this will detract from your scores.

Kori Stevens

Make sure you have competent backup dancers that you can depend on...people who are dedicated to you, both on AND off stage. Props should be sturdy and well put together. The slightest mishap can make world of difference.

Joey Jay

Back up dancers should be... DANCERS. Don't go ask your friends because it is easier. If you want to win, it takes some time and it's an investment. Have real dancers work with you on your routine, and once it's finished, clean, clean, clean. If it's precise, it's beautiful.

Freddy Prinze Charming

If you're going to use props, making sure they look professional is key. They should look as though thought and effort were put into creating and building them. If you have smaller props like microphones, make sure they get used during your number. Backup dancers should be polished and in sync with costumes that show as much effort as yours.

AJ Menendez

You will only have a few moments to set up and break down. Make sure your props can be put on the stage and removed quickly and easily. When using back up dancers, make sure they are all on point and don't upstage you. Biggest mistake with that is when you're back up dancers either upstage your performance or damage the quality of it.

Jayden Knight

Make sure that none of your props are broken or not secure. Ensure your dancers know the routine and have lots of practice.

Natasha Richards

K.I.S.S. Keep it simple stupid! I learned that while teaching ballroom dancing at the Arthur Murray Dance Studio.

Ty Nolan

Be prepared by making all props user friendly that does not require a lot of setup time. Make them with the same attention to detail as your costume. Make sure your dancers do not distract from or outshine your performance and they know their routine as well as you knows yours biggest mistake: poor quality props, backup dancers/performers not in unison when they are supposed to be.

Gage Gatlyn

Props and Backup Dancers are allowed during Creative Costuming Talent and Final Night Talent. Biggest mistake: The stage looking like a clustered mess. Practice your choreography with your backups, A LOT. Take the time to make sure your props are realistic and/or clean, and make sure your set matches your number and costuming.

**"It's a good thing I was born a girl, otherwise
I'd be a drag queen."**
Dolly Parton

Chapter Seven

Transition through "Wardrobe Changes"

UNEDITED RESPONSES

Amy DeMilo

Have all your categories in order and together from costume, jewels, to shoes.. big mistake not being organized...

DeyJzah Opulent Mirage

When doing wardrobe changes either by yourself or with another person(s) just knowing where things go, how they are applied and how they come off are the biggest things that you need to know

Brittany Moore

Make sure your changes are functional and make sense

Anson Reign

I love wardrobe changes during a number - it's something a contestant can do by themselves and it usually doesn't require other people or back up dancers, and it can change the entire feel of a number and raise the bar. A common mistake is making it too complex and missing cues. Also, make sure you can't see the 2nd costume underneath your first one.

Coco Montrese

Wardrobe changes have a very professional dresser whose main concern is you and not everything else going on around you. Find someone who doesn't mine watching the pageant when it comes out on DVD not while it's going on.

Vinnie Marconi

A good DRESSER is a very IMPORTANT person for you backstage. They should think like you, be one-step ahead of you in your needs, have an acute eye for detail, and have PRACTICED getting you ready so if there is a "wardrobe malfunction" they are prepared to handle it. Have your 'emergency kit' well stocked with everything from needle & thread to hairspray, and ANYTHING else that could fall off, pop off, rip, stain... Murphy's Law strikes quite often when getting ready for a pageant. The FIVE P's was introduced to me by one of my first sponsors, Kamden Cass, "Proper Preparation Prevents Poor Performance" and BOY does that hold true!

Note by The Infamous Todd Kachinski Kottmeier: This popular drag term comes from the seven "P's" made famous decades ago by the British Military's slogan, "Proper Planning and Preparation Prevents Piss Poor Performance.

Denise Russell

Hire a good dresser. Make sure that you have emergency supplies! Needle and thread, duct tape and glue. Have all your changes lined up on the clothes rack in order. Make your costume change first, then do your make-up touch-ups. It is a pageant; don't be late.

Vivika D'Angelo

"Tear-away clothing" is a big issue. Some are not taken off smoothly making it look like a mess.

Sam Hare

Please practice multiple times any wardrobe changes in a talent. Multiple times! If you are off of the stage for more than 30 seconds at the most it is too long. Make sure there is a plan for where you or others will change the costume and again make sure there is lots of practice. That is the biggest mistake often made.

Breonna Tenae

Keep your wardrobe to a minimum with every thing organized. Keep your shoes, jewelry, accessories, hair, and with the correct outfit. Ensure you outfit is steamed and flaw free ready for each category in order. Hire a dresser to keep them in order for you. All you have to do is stand there and let them put you in and out of costumes. Make sure you do practice runs so you will always be ready on point for each category. We all know things can happen unexpectedly. Keep mending tools and products for quick fixes (pins, glue, tape, adhesives, sewing needles, and thread). Always be prepared for mishaps!

Stephanie Stuart

I place my clothes in the order i will need then in competition then your not searching or digging around things are right there for you all lined up.

Rico Taylor

Practice, practice, and practice before taking it on stage we all know stuff happens and issues arise best thing you can do is play it off like you meant to do it or like it was part or it never stop what your doing and freak out try your hardest to work threw it.

Tori Taylor

Choose clothes that require the same undergarments, as you have no time to be re-bodying.

Darryl Kent

My biggest pet peeve with costume changes are cover-ups that are either too short, don't have closures, or don't cover the costume below. The entire purpose is to cover-up what is below, which means it should not allow the judges or audience to see ANY part of anything below... (Sleeve, fringe, etc)

Taina T Norell

Know the timing on your mix. Rehearse it until you're tired of listening to it!

Jay Santana

Wardrobe changes are an integral part of any pageant. The wardrobe/costume changes require a lot of work and timing. It is very important that the contestant know exactly what clothing, accessories, hair, etc. they need at what point in the pageant. It is also imperative that the contestant have a dressing assistant that is very organized. The biggest issue or mistake that I have seen contestants struggle with in relation to wardrobe changes is failing to prepare for unforeseen situations-a broken zipper, missing sequins on a gown, a forgotten tie.

Jayden Knight

Make sure they are clean cut and no make up on any of your outfits and nothing is lost because you will lose points.

Mykul Jay Valentine

Have everything prepared and on the same hanger days before your pageant. That way it is much easier for your dresser to help you out. And you always want a experienced dresser who can make you laugh and calm you down.

Dana Douglas

All your changes, including hair must be rehearsed and timed. You usually have 15 to 20 minutes tops at national pageants. Hire a Veteran Dresser, who does hair and all dressing details...

Jennifer Foxx

Only use a wardrobe change when it is unexpected. I never give points for the obvious. Timing is everything and the element of surprise can be valuable to a contestant.

Mis Sadistic

I feel very strongly about this; you should always be able to dress yourself when it comes to wardrobe. If you have people helping you and there not there, sometimes you are alone for what ever reason you must be able to get ready by yourself. If you are called up next to go on stage half dressed because your dresser was in the bathroom won't cut it. When it is your turn to go on, that's it no second chances. Remember to always have your costumes organized and ready to go, in order of the categories, if not that is one mistake you usually can't bounce back from.

Freddy Prinze Charming

Any costume changes should be seamless and smooth. They should never take you away from the stage for too long.

AJ Menendez

This is where dressers come in handy. While you're on stage doing one category, your dresser should be back stage setting up the outfit and things you will need for the next one so that you can change quickly and easily. It's helpful if you change your facial hair for each category (Use hair gel or hairspray rather than glue to make this easier) it shows diversity. The biggest mistake is to go into a competition without a dresser and thinking you can easily do it on your own. Having a good dresser relieves some of the stress.

Joey Jay

Be fast; don't make such a production of a costume/wardrobe change. The longer it takes to change, the bigger and better the judges expect it to be.

Natasha Richards

The categories must be planned before, and the gays must have their jobs; Hair, Makeup and gown zip. It's not the dress, it's the hanger that matters.

Ty Nolan
You need a dresser with the knowledge of your wardrobe.

Gage Gatlyn

I feel that if a contestant does not know how to handle wardrobe changes throughout the contest, pageants may not be the contest for them, just yet.

**"People that never believe
the right shoes make a difference,
Never watched Cinderella."**
The Infamous Todd Kachinski Kottmeier

Chapter Eight

"Makeup, Hair, and Shoes"

UNEDITED RESPONSES

Bob Taylor

These are essential to success. All accessories should match and/or be appropriate for the clothing chosen. Hair and make up are very important too. Biggest mistakes are not going over the details with a fine toothed comb (no pun intended).

Amy DeMilo

Either you can do it alone or hire help....

DeyJzah Opulent Mirage

Makeup hair and shoes should never be dowdy, uncombed, ashy or tarnished, unless you are presenting something that calls for this type of look.

Brittany Moore.

Everything matters. Make sure your makeup is well blended and current and the hair is clean shinny polished.

Anastacia Dupree

CLEAN, CLEAN, CLEAN... is all I can say make sure everything is blended and your hair is smoothed out for any updo's.

Anson Reign

Look slick. All the time. Make sure your facial hair blends well into your real hair line, and make sure your jaw/face is well defined. A mistake often made by Kings is that they feel less masculine if they wear make-up. Not the cast. Wear it, use it, and perfect it. Don't shy away from something that can help you better your illusion.

Denise Russell

All of your wigs, nails, heels and lashes should be NEW! Too often Queens wear wigs that look like they have been drug behind the car on the way to the pageant!

Vinnie Marconi

I was under the impression to be a MALE illusionist, thinking make-up wasn't necessary... WRONG! To make a brow bushier, to have a more defined jaw line, to have ABS, it is essential! YES, you use the same theatrical make-up as the queens because under REAL pageant lights (not just a house spotlight) you will be completely washed out if you choose the 'natural' look! A large amount of facial hair isn't necessary, just be absolutely CERTAIN it follows your jaw line/lip-line. You ARE allowed to spruce up your shoes with 'bling!' Always keep in mind the hem-line of your pants when choosing shoes. A pair of lifts so you are taller compared to your back-ups will NOT work with those jeans fitted for sneakers!

Coco Montrese

Every element when competing is important. Make up hair and shoes all complete the package; biggest mistake is thinking that one is more important than the other they all contribute to a complete look.

Stephanie Stuart

All of these items need to appear as if you are wearing them for the first time. Clean smooth and classy!

Vivika D'Angelo

Color coordinating is a big issue. Looking to see what colors fit you better and if you should wear your hair up or down depends on the gown itself

Sam Hare

Make-up needs to be stage ready, paint for the spotlight and not the dressing room. Hair should be neat and in place, that is a big problem with talent and evening gown hair. Shoes should be clean, in good repair, and in gown they should match the gown color or a slightly darker shade on the gown. They should fit also and the contestant should have practiced walking in the shoes.

Rico Taylor

Make sure everything matches your skin tone. Make sure the hair matches. You must match all outfits if you have blonde hair, your facial hair shouldn't be black or red. Best thing to do is make sure everything is very neat and clean.

Breonna Tenae

Choose make up that showcase your beauty. Never over do make up in a pageant. Keep it clean and make sure all accents do not over power anything. Keep all accessories just that, "Accessories." Many go over board with jewelry and trimmings. It makes their package gaudy. Keep it to a minimum. You don't need rings on every finger. If your earrings are super big, you don't need a huge necklace. If your gown is stoned and high neck, you don't need to lay jewelry on top of it keep it elegant and clean

Darryl Kent

Hair secured; use called wig bond and bobby pins. Makeup should be tasteful and relevant. Shoes should be POLISHED.

Tori Taylor

Do not copy last year's winner, get your own

Anson Reign

Look slick. All the time. Make sure your facial hair blends well into your real hair line, and make sure your jaw/face is well defined. A mistake often made by Kings is that they feel less masculine if they wear make-up. Not the case! Wear it, use it, perform in it.

Joey Jay

Invest, invest, invest. Shoes and makeup should always compliment the look, and the concept. Hair should always be secure. This is illusion, so you want to make sure that you keep the illusion as believable as possible. Once the hair comes off, you are now a man. Oops.

Tiffani Middlesexx

Wear make up that is becoming to your face.

Taina T Norell

Keep it clean , a lot of girls think the more they have on stage the better lies & fairy tales. It's all about coordination.

Jay Santana

When an entertainer makes it to a pageant, their hair, makeup, and shoes must be phenomenal. Everything should come together into an amazing package in each facet of the pageant. The biggest mistakes include fly-alway hair, uneven haircut, makeup that runs, scuffs on shoes.

Jayden Knight

Make sure everything is clean cut and fixed as proper as it can be. If things look messy you will lose points.

Natasha Richards

Find someone comfortable and trustworthy, who will always look you in the eye when giving you your kudos for your great look. A dress/gown that is to short or to long and scuffed shoes is very common mistakes.

Ty Nolan

Again you need someone with the knowledge of hair and makeup. Your shoes should be new, not be scuffed.

Mykul Jay Valentine

For boys, there's not much you can do. You never want to wear too much makeup, and look fake. You want to keep it as natural as possible. It may be a beauty pageant, but you still have to be a man. Even if you are doing some crazy makeup for your talent, make sure it's not too "draggy" keep it masculine.

Dana Douglas

Never buy the shoes or accessories before the actual outfit is in your hands! I have a closet full of shoes that I never got to use because the color didn't match the finished outfit...Wasted money.

Jennifer Foxx

You are being judged as women, not manikins, not fantasies, but actual images of women. Much of female impersonation is hyper sized. TRY to keep it as realistic as possible.

Mis Sadistic

When it comes to makeup be very organized and have back ups just incase a tip should break on a liner pencil or lipstick should hit the floor. That goes for extra lash glue as well. In the case of hair, excuse the pun, but your hair should be kept in a case. This will insure no damage come to it and the piece will be ready to wear when you need it. You should not be trying to style a hair piece minutes before going on stage. Shoes are a very special item when it comes to drag. This is not an item easily replaced, say a shoe breaks or is lost. Always, always bring at least one backup pair; something that can go with all your outfits. Your shoes should fit well so you are able to move with ease and grace. They should be broken in" and comfortable to walk in. Your toes should not be hanging off the front because a shoe is to small or a heel off the back. "

Freddy Prinze Charming

From talent to eveningwear, attention needs to be paid to these three things. Shoes should be clean, especially for eveningwear. Time should be taken to do hair and makeup is flawless, and fit your talent or eveningwear theme.

AJ Menendez

Unless your numbers require you to look like a hot mess, than don't. Make sure your hair, facial hair is as they should be with no untrimmed hair or any out of place. Shoes should be polished at all times.

Gage Gatlyn

I feel that if a contestant does not know how to do his own hair or make-up or match his shoes, pageants may not be the contest for them, just yet.

**"Dancers are
athletes of God."**
Albert Einstein

Chapter Nine

"Song Selection, Dancing, and Movement"

UNEDITED RESPONSES

Bob Taylor

Song selection comes down to a matter of taste. Contestants are not judged on their selection as much as they are on how they delivered the music to the audience and judges.

Amy DeMilo

Know your words and routine; never let anyone on your team outshine you on stage.

DeyJzah Opulent Mirage

Songs are your choice, knowing your audience is a good guide, but at the end of the day it's your choice. I love to do song that I connect with and can interpret on stage. See talent to understand condition and movement.

Brittany Moore

Movement should flow and every step has a reason; move sensibly.

Denise Russell

Know yourself, does the voice you are going to lip sync, sound like it would come out of you. Practice your modeling and you stage movements! Be graceful! Try to be your most feminine!

Vinnie Marconi

Choice of music & mix will make or break a performer. I look for something that I can REALLY pull the judges in with, something to tug on their heartstrings, make them dance in their seats, or laugh until they pee. Make sure the costume is a COSTUME, and matches the story the music tells. Try to use as much of the stage as possible, EVERYONE wants to see you, but remember, it's the JUDGES with the score sheets.

Coco Montrese

Make sure you pick music and choreography that you are capable of doing. This is very important; hiring professional dancers doesn't mean a sure win, especially if you can't keep up with them yourself. You are the front and center everything else around you should compliment you not overpower you.

Anson Reign

Pick a song that you feel passionate about. A common mistake a contestant can make is picking a song they think" the judges want to see. If you don't feel awesome about it.

Vivika D'Angelo

Many dancers as I have seen, start off with a slow intro making an impact on when the big number begin. I- you start big you need to end with a bang.

Natasha Richards

Not knowing the words to your music is one of the biggest mistakes. Know how to move to your selection. Know them and love them, even if your song selection and movements are the same. People, (your fans) come to see that. Now make it your best.

Sam Hare

Song selection should be within the time limit, be of quality, mixed well (not homemade), and not have an abrupt ending. The contestant should have the right timing when entering the stage, and movement needs to be in flow or rhythm of the song. If you are using a microphone, continue to stay in character and use the microphone throughout the number.

Breonna Tenae

Music selection is left up to the performer but when choosing your music make sure you have a vision and you can bring that vision to life onstage. Whatever music you choose it has to be entertaining and hold the judges attention. don't do overly boring over done talents keep it fresh and spread your surprises through the whole talent it should build and build until you raise the roof off of the venue and leave everyone on their feet wanting more but remember its not the crowd with the pen and paper its those 3-4 people on the judges panel. Know your words points make always have fun during talent we want to see you enjoy performing for us! one of the biggest mistakes is that contestants feel they must not perform their talent publicly until after the pageant NOT TRUE give a few test runs to see how the crowd respond have some one to video it make improvements be for you take it to competition.

Dana Douglas

If you can't dance, don't use professional dancers that are going to out dance you. Know your limitations and your strengths and design a talent that showcases you at your best.

Rico Taylor

Variety is always great but something's you stick with your niche especially if your great at it. It's a pageant, but doing a mix of different thing to show diversity is amazing. Make sure you do a mix with costumes that work. Ensure the props, dance routine, and dancers all work. One wrong thing could hurt your points.

Darryl Kent

Make sure your movements have purpose and are fluid. Just don't move to the side of the stage for the sake of moving, use the musicality you have to develop subtle movements that have purpose. Song selection is the key. There are billions of songs in the public domain; don't be a copycat. Also, there are billions of songs by men and billions of songs by women. Whatever gender you are portraying, chose music by that gender.

Jennifer Foxx

Make a musical selection that looks as though it could be delivered by what we as judges see before us onstage....example: Small white queens pantomiming Patti Labelle is inconsistent as is larger African-American performers doing Taylor Swift. Make us believe what we see, since your TOTAL illusion is what is being judged.

Tori Taylor

Don't do songs that are bigger than your talent. Stay in your comfort zone.

Tiffani Middlesexx

Song selection is important. Pick something you're comfortable with.

Jayden Knight

Do something that you are comfortable with. If you do something your not, you will likely to mess up.

Taina T Norell

If you're not feeling the song, most likely your not going to be comfortable on stage and it will show. When you're selecting a song to perform as your talent, you must feel each minute down your body and soul to the point that it reflects and radiates.

Jay Santana

Selection of song, choreography and use of the stage are all important. When judging, I expect to see something new and fresh-- not something I've seen a contestant do at five prior pageants or watched fifteen other performers do. One of the biggest mistakes I have seen is a contestant failing to scope out the actual stage that t hey will be performing on.

Mykul Jay Valentine

Pick a song that you actually LIKE and can listen to over and over. Don't just do something because someone tells you to. You want to be able to "feel" what you are doing because it really doesn't translate on stage. And be sure to use the entire stage.

Mis Sadistic

Some of the biggest mistakes happen before you even hit the pageant stage. Girls you must pick music that fits you and your ability to move and move with it gracefully. You and your music should be paired like a perfect romance. Weather it is fast or slow you need to be able to move and dance to it without struggling to keep up with it. When it comes to music selection take a long look at yourself in the proverbial mirror and know you limitations so your performance will be one you can be proud of.

Freddy Prinze Charming

Song selection should be something you know you can perform well. Not something chosen last minute, some thought should have been put into it. Any dancing and movement will always look best if choreographed, simply to avoid the pacing that can happen when there is no choreography.

AJ Menendez

Song selection can be pretty tricky. The one thing I can say for sure is that you should not have any profanity in your songs at all. It's been my own experience that when your talent number sends an important message, it's a winner. Not all entertainers do the same; it's to each entertainer's discretion. Your talent number should not be any more than 6 to 7 minutes long, make sure you check with the promoters if you are unsure. Choose a song you are passionate about, it helps because it shows on stage.

Joey Jay

Look at the stage and study it before you perform. See the size, how wide it is, the length, etc. Are there steps? You need to utilize the entire stage. It shows that you are confident and comfortable with yourself.

Natasha Richards

Not knowing the words to your music is one of the biggest mistakes. Know how to move to your selection. Know them and love them, even if your song selection and movements are the same. People, (your fans) come to see that. Now make it your best.

Ty Nolan

Know how to dance, know the routine, make it classy, and not trashy.

Darryl Kent

Make sure your movements have purpose and are fluid. Just don't move to the side of the stage for the sake of moving. Use the musicality. You have to develop subtle movements that have purpose. Song selection is the key. There are billions of songs.

Stephanie Stuart

I tend to do solo talents, however I remind you to make sure your dancers out dance you!

**"We gain strength, and courage, and confidence
By each experience in which we really stop to
look fear in the face... we must do that which
we think we cannot."**
Eleanor Roosevelt

Chapter Ten

Realizing the moment
"You are ready to compete"

UNEDITED RESPONSES

Darryl Kent

You should have a desire to represent any title you compete for, not just to have a crown. Study the system and find the system(s) that play to your strengths. Study scoring systems and see what categories are more highly weighed so you have a fair chance at winning every time you hit the stage.

Bob Taylor

This is a matter of choice. Pick a system that caters to your abilities and knowledge. For example, there are now pageants for newcomers, seasoned and over 40 years of age.

Amy DeMilo

When you feel like your ready to or just the simple wanting to win. Anytime is good, as you always learn....

DeyJzah Opulent Mirage

For some it is never time to compete, but for those that feel like you want to or have to its when you and only when after you have studied what you are actually competing for

Brittany Moore

Preparation perfect practice makes perfect.

Vivika D'Angelo

Best time to compete is when you feel you're ready. No one is born ready, we build as we go along it's an amazing ride win or lose.

Vinnie Marconi

I've been asked to compete in a couple of pageants now that my response was, "I'm not ready." There is a LOT to learn to be GOOD at the art of illusion. I've had the honor to watch a National Competition and my little pea-brain can't even conceive the brilliance and perfection I saw on that stage! Since I don't even have a full year under my belt, I am still awestruck by the caliber of performers in that level of competition. Maybe one day...

Coco Montrese

Pay attention to every detail, you know you are ready to compete when you are financially, physically, mentally and emotionally stable. Everything is to your liking and your vision of what you've created is complete.

Denise Russell

If you are competing on the National level, you need to have nerves of steel to exude confidence! You must command the stage. It takes money to compete. If a pageant is going to break you, don't do it!

Jayden Knight

The time to compete is when you are ready. Do not push yourself because you are less likely to succeed. Have confidence in yourself and stay positive.

Sam Hare

The qualities of the best candidates are organization, planning, follow-through, preparation, and investing in the package. Know the system, trust the system or do not compete, and understand what is needed to win. Expect big competition and prepare for big competition. Performers not ready to compete are those that are not focused and ready for all categories. They do not have the help or resources to compete, or they are just competing to be onstage. The time to compete is when you have studied the system, are prepared to win and prepared to reign.

Anastacia Dupree

The time to compete for a pageant is when you are polished and ready to walk on stage. Many of the best have helpers at a pageant but remember those people don't help them every show just that night. You need to be able to do that every time you walk on stage or anytime you are booked somewhere.

Dana Douglas

If you see a girl win a pageant, and you know that you could have been better, it's time to compete! If you sit around wishing that that celebrity was you, it's time to compete! If you feel that you have something to offer our community, it's time to compete! If you want more respect from your piers and respect for yourself, it's time to compete!

Taina T Norell

When you're financially stable, with the right sponsors, and you have your act together.

Stephanie Stuart

When you can afford to lose, you're ready to compete!

Rico Taylor

When you feel you have reached a point to we're you have the knowledge, costuming, and mixing skills. Practice on microphone. It was two years before I entered my first pageant. I asked my drag mom before I went that route.

AJ Menendez

Before you should even think about competing, you should perfect your skills in the craft of Male Illusion. Learn from older MI's, don't be afraid to ask questions and perfect your craft.

Breonna Tenae

Time to compete is when you have the self confidence to walk out there and do it like a professional there should be no self doubt! You want it go for it but make sure you have the package complete before you go up for judging. Stay humble you can't win them all use smaller pageants and learning venues to build your package and make it stronger. Take head to comments judges presented to you on the score sheets. and PLEASE DO NOT ACT A FOOL if you don't win. Be gracious and courteous at all times! So should your team that is with you!

Tori Taylor

Compete when you are self sufficient, if you can't get yourself ready daily, you are not ready to represent

Tiffani Middlesexx

Compete when you feel its time to compete.

Jay Santana

The right time to compete is when the CONTESTANT feels secure AND polished enough to do so.

Mykul Jay Valentine

Simple. The time to compete is when you are ready. Wait until you have the time and money. Don't go in "half-assed."

Jennifer Foxx

It depends on the venue you are competing in and at what point you are in on your progression as an artist. Do not overload your plate, HOWEVER always keep in mind, "If you come with an open mind to a bigger opportunity you can learn volumes just being there. All experience in theater is good experience."

Freddy Prinze Charming

Being ready to compete often depends on the type of pageant you're competing in. When you're still a new performer, it's always a good idea to get experience, in both performing and competing before jumping into a bigger pageant. Many performers don't feel they're ready to compete until they've been entertaining for several years. If you are honest with yourself about the level you are at in terms of performance, you'll know when you're ready to compete and in what type of pageant.

Mis Sadistic

I feel with all my heart if you feel you are ready, than it is time for you to begin competing. This like all other processes in life is a learning experience. I would like to follow that up by saying you must be able to take constructive criticism and use it to better yourself. By entering a pageant you are asking to be judged, keep that in mind.

Natasha Richards

When you feel like you are not letting yourself down. The audience loves you, now make them smile. When you can do that you know it's time and it's right.

Ty Nolan

Competing requires confidence, preparation, dedication, money and time...a lack of any of the above lowers your chances.

Gage Gatlyn

Contestants should not compete for Master Male Illusionist if they are not ready to uphold the highest of standards as a performance artist and Titleholder.

Joey Jay

Compete when you have nothing else to improve. Take your best package, every time.

Anson Reign

When you can't stop thinking about it and you want it more than you want anything else - that's when it's time to compete. If you only want something shiny to wear on your head, don't compete. Go by yourself a crown. You have to want to EARN it, earn the title and earn the respect, not just have the crown.

**"If you believe others will win;
you are right."**
The Infamous Todd Kachinski Kottmeier

Chapter Eleven

What do you recommend to entertainers entering a pageant already including a performer considered to be, "Favored to Win?"

UNEDITED RESPONSES

Bob Taylor

Do your homework, focus on the goal at hand, and always be yourself and not try to be someone else.

Amy DeMilo

Bring a gun to the knife fight! All anyone can do is their best so put your best foot forward and go....

DeyJzah Opulent Mirage

I recommend two things. I recommend they listen to their heart and follow their dreams.

Brittany Moore

Show up. You never know, it could be your night (and that's not always the case that someone is favored).

Vinnie Marconi

BRING IT! Even the 'favored' are subject to Murphy's Law. If you don't have the full package and can pull it off seamlessly (notice I didn't say effortlessly) you won't take away the crown. You do take away the constructive criticism to help you learn and grow for the next one!

Coco Montrese

Never under estimate anyone in the competition. If you are favorite to win, don't become relaxed and think that it's just going to happen because just when you do you find yourself competing for the same title the following year.

Denise Russell

Do your homework. Leave nothing to chance. Do not get caught up in the dram. Get plenty of sleep. The more you are prepared, the better your chances of winning!

Anson Reign

Anything can happen. That person who is "favored to win" could fall of the stage. Be confident, but don't be over-confident, and don't be arrogant. Be gracious to the rest of the contestants as well as to the judges. Go with an open mind.

Vivika D'Angelo

I don't believe in "the favored to win." You need to go in with your mind set as a winner regardless of where you place.

Sam Hare

The first advice is that anyone can be beaten, and if you as a contestant believe the 'big name' contestant will be crowned please save your money for a fair pageant. Prepare, prepare, prepare and be ready to battle anyone that shows up. Focus on your package only and don't play mind games with yourself.

Anastacia Dupree

Be yourself and bring the best package you can. But remember there is only one winner. That doesn't make you any less able to win just bring it.

Stephanie Stuart

Don't listen to the talkers. Do your thing and if you have done your best that's all you can do all we have to be in life is yourself!

Rico Taylor

Never confuse cocky with confidence. Remember who you are and where you came from. Don't get a big head, as it will be a big down fall. Its okay to feel good about yourself and confident, but don't go in like the other contestants are jokes. Be respectful, humble, and give them your best.

Breonna Tenae

Go in it and give your best. Take notes and learn. Pageants are great learning tools to make you a better performer. Remember, even if someone else is favored to win you can always change the judges mind. Give them your all and let them know you are there to win! Even if you don't win, you will be remembered!

Tiffani Middlesexx

Just go out and do your best.

Darryl Kent

Anyone can be beaten on any night. You have to always be mature enough to accept the opinion of 7 total strangers and act accordingly before and after crowning. We all have been at pageants when the results might have been suspect, but it is just as important to carry yourself gracefully in defeat as it is with humility in victory.

Tori Taylor

Cross your "T's" and dot your "I's." There are no small details.

Taina T Norell

Practice makes perfect. Anyone can be beat at a pageant.

Jay Santana

Always remember that no matter how good you are, there is always someone as good as, if not better, than you are.

Mykul Jay Valentine

Anyone can be beaten. Just make sure you are prepared. Never go in thinking, "I have this…"

Dana Douglas

Their have always been and will always be, "favored girls," usually because they are the seasoned veterans. But any of us can and have been beaten. Don't be afraid to lose.

Jennifer Foxx

Preparation, meeting opportunity, equals success. Bring your best and present; from there it is out of your control....

Mis Sadistic

When you enter a pageant there is always some kind of talk of who is the favored one. Ignore it.

Freddy Prinze Charming

Do your best. There are no guarantees.

AJ Menendez

Go into this with confidence but NEVER be cocky. As good as you may be there is always someone better. Have fun with it and learn from it win or loose.

Joey Jay

Beat the politics. Make sure that your package is so impressive, that the politics have no chance at beating your package. Even if the politics did win, there would be an uproar with the audience and the system, making it visible to everyone**Jayden Knight**

Don't let them get you down. Always keep in mind if you don't win you learned something from it.

Joey Jay

Beat the politics. Make sure that your package is so impressive, that the politics have no chance at beating your package. Even if the politics did win, there would be an uproar with the audience and the system, making it visible to everyone that the system itself favors some over others... hurting the systems reputation. That's the last thing the system owner wants.

Natasha Richards

Everyone can be beat. The favorite is you! If you do not feel taht then you shouldn't enter.

Ty Nolan

Be prepared and expect the unexpected... no one is a winner until the numbers and opinions of the judges are tabulated.

Gage Gatlyn

Contestant's talent numbers are available for review by the judges if questions are called... Think of it as Instant Replay." There is no room for favoritism in Master MI and those judges will surely get "Called Out" if they were to try.

**"There are two kinds of people,
Those who do the work
and those who take the credit.
Try to be in the first group;
there is less competition there."**
Indira Gandhi

Chapter Thirteen

"Competitor's Edge"

UNEDITED RESPONSES

Dana Douglas

Get out there and make a name for yourself. Be a good entertainer, professional and on time. Be a likeable and sober person that people want to be around and to hire.

Anastacia Dupree

Study the system and learn what they are looking for, prepare your self months before don't wait till last min to start getting ready.

Amy DeMilo

Save money, tackle one category at a time. Practice routine repeatedly, have everything in order, and ready before you go to compete. Preparation is everything...

DeyJzah Opulent Mirage

Find your Uniqueness, display your ESTEEM, Bang out you Promotion, and Brush up on the pageants history and creed, and be mindful of your off stage behavior.

Jay Santana

Be professional at ALL TIMES. Stay away from the drag drama and politics. Avoid feeding into the gossip. Be respectful of all the promoters and other contestants. Remember that please, thank you, and excuse me go a long way!

Stephanie Stuart

Practice, practice, and practice your walk in an evening gown. Practice your presentation speech. Get coached on questions. Practice the talent category.

Rico Taylor

Costuming, talent knowing words, playing the crowd and finding your niche. Always be thankful.

Brittany Moore

Preparation, practice, knowledge, readiness, and assertive.

Coco Montrese

To give yourself an edge on all the other contestants, you need to prepare, focus, physically train, make sure finance is in order, and relax before competing , save all energy for the actual competition.

Vinnie Marconi

1. Think about what SERVICE you can do with that crown. It will help in the On-Stage Interview. 2. Have your clothes fit to PERFECTION, ALL of them! 3. RECITE your talent words and when you practice them, FEEL the meaning, take note of EVERY hesitation and breath. 4. Don't think you can do it all yourself. Ask close friends to 'preview,' suggest, and help with what you have in your head to develop a whole package. 5. Remember the 5 P's ~ Proper Preparation Prevents Poor Performance!

Denise Russell

Have everything ready to go weeks before the competition. Have your talent number well rehearsed. Make sure that everything is paid for, before the pageant. Do not concern yourself with what the other contestants are bringing to the pageant. During the days of competition, build in some quiet time, where you can decompress.

Anson Reign

1. Create a neat, professional, nice looking Facebook page or website. 2. Only put up videos and pictures that make you look wonderful - not drunken pictures of you partying at the bar on your birthday. 3. Practice the songs you are considering doing for a pageant.

Vivika D'Angelo

Plan ahead. Make a list of every category. Make sure you have everything for each even the basics like nails, jewelry, hair, shoes, nylons, padding if you wear them.

Sam Hare

(1) Study the system and read the category descriptions, (2) get organized as you plan your package, (3) invest in yourself and find others willing to invest as well, (4) spend time and energy into being ready for any competition when you walk into registration, and (5) practice, practice, practice!

Bob Taylor

Preparation. Rehearse. Set a budget and stick to it

Taina T Norell

Stay focus on you. Stop looking around to see who's wearing what or wearing the most sickening gown. It creates tension and distracts from your package.

Breonna Tenae

Learn your strengths and use them to your advantage. May performers do not know their strengths you have to watch your self on video ask your audience for suggestions learn what the people like from you then perfect that!

Natasha Richards

1). The story must be told. The people in the story (aka) back up dancers, make up artists, hairdressers, etc., mapped out. 2). Sponsorship is imperative. Gather people that believe in your story/success. 3) Mind set- You Are Going to Win. Never think of the other contestants as hard as that may be. 4. Don't forget Zanax. 5. Take care of your team, see # 1, you are nothing without them.

Tori Taylor

Chose carefully, get qualified backstage help, practice your talent, review interview skills.

Mis Sadistic

Five things a contestant can do to prepare for a pageant long before you get to compete in one would be: Study the pageants, by this I mean look at the past winners and there performances. Study how they handle themselves on question and answer. If you know someone that has won a title or are able to talk with a girl that has won a title. Don't be afraid to ask questions. Listen to what they have to say, the key is listen to them. Take what they have to say and apply it to yourself. Go to pageants as a spectator; see what they are like and what goes on in the course of a pageant. Pay attention to how the girls carry themselves during all the categories. Be prepared financially for everything that comes with being in a pageant. Entry fee, transportation, hotel, costuming, food, and the list can go on. You could be a helper for one of the pageant girls and get a real first hand look at what goes on behind the scenes. This would be your biggest learning experience and most beneficial.

Darryl Kent

1. Know yourself. Your strengths, your weaknesses, your limitations. 2. Prepare a package specifically for a system you specifically want to represent instead of a catch-all generic package. 3. Separate your friends from your fans and be mature enough to accept criticism.

Tiffani Middlesexx

I don't know if there is any edge.

Joey Jay

1. Put it on paper. Brainstorm many ideas and see where they go. Do not be inspired by other acts you have seen in the past, for they are no longer original. 2. Ask, ask, and ask. There is nothing wrong with asking questions, in fact, it makes you more personable, and builds a good relationship with others. 3. Be aware of who you ask. Whether you like it or not, the best winning advice you can get is of course from a winner. They have done it, they know the ropes, so save yourself some time and go ask as many winners as possible. 4. Be humble. Never bad mouth, for you never know whose ears are in range. Always be thankful and ready to help someone else out who may be a worse situation that yours. 5. Have an open mind. You never know who may come out of the woodwork. Something can always happen. 6. Just for giggles, here is one more. BE ON TIME. It shows that your responsible, professional, and have a desire to succeed. If you are just one minute late, you have already given first place to someone else.

Jennifer Foxx

The winning edge inherently lies in your team. Hire the best artists at their craft. If there is someone that knows more than you know about any subject. Enlist them. Surround yourself with the best in the industry and in your personal life; hose that love you want you to succeed.

Freddy Prinze Charming

Work on perfecting everything: your lip-sync, your modeling, your choreography, costume changes, interview and on-stage question. You can never over practice" something.

Ty Nolan

1) Prepare, 2) research, 3) practice, 4) practice, and 5) practice

Gage Gatlyn

Always do the right thing... ALWAYS. Why reach for the moon when you can touch the stars? Always think as a professional. Always think on a National Level. Always believe that YOU are a WINNER! "

AJ Menendez

1. Don't do a pageant last minute; give yourself time to put together a winning package. Never just slap together a package. 2. When you've chosen the pageant you want to do, learn all there is to learn about it. 3. Work on your presentation speech as soon as possible and give yourself time to learn it. 4. Give yourself time to play with different songs so that you can choose the best one for you. 5. Try not to second guess yourself too much.

Jayden Knight

1.) Practice your song and dance 2.)Find out who the judges are so you can prepare yourself for their questions and what they look for 3.) Prepare a flawless outfit 4.) Get a dresser and hairstylist 5.) Practice interview questions.

More DRAG Tips from famous entertainers are in this 10 Black Book Series.

Book 2

Book 4

Book 8

**"Judges ought to be more leaned than witty,
more reverent than plausible, and more advised than confident.
Above all things, integrity is their portion and proper virtue."**
Francis Bacon

Chapter Thirteen

Qualities of a "Fair Judge"

UNEDITED RESPONSES

Bob Taylor

Integrity; non bias, the ability to judge based on what they see that night versus what they have seen the contestant do in other venues or competitions

Amy DeMilo

Honesty and to be unbiased.

DeyJzah Opulent Mirage

Competence, unbiased, and experience in the art form can make a judge fair

Brittany Moore

Open minded with a knowledge of the pageants.

Vinnie Marconi

Knowledgeable about the criteria for each category, be able to set aside prior issues with a contestant aside to "SEE" that night's performance on its own. The judge needs an open mind to what the contestants are bringing, with no preconceived notions or expectations. They need to believe in the system, its crown, and what it means to the community and the art.

Coco Montrese

Qualities of a fair judge, is consistency. Always have a reason for your score, look at every contestant the same. Give them all the same treatment even if their name is established or they are a newcomer. Make yourself available to all contestants following any competition.

Denise Russell

A judge needs to have great knowledge of Drag. A judge needs to 'judge' what they only see that evening.

Anson Reign

A judge needs to be professional, impartial, and well informed about the categories and how to judge each category.

Vivika D'Angelo

A judge should judge you for that day. If he or she knows you and knows what you have done in the past should not reflect or make any difference on what they are judging you on that night.

Darryl Kent

Educated in the craft, knowledgeable in all genres of music, open minded, and sober.

Sam Hare

A fair judge needs to understand the system, what the promoter is looking for. They need to know how to appropriately score contestants. Judges need to have plenty of positive and negative feedback for all contestants as well. Judges need to keep an open mind, pay attention to detail, refrain from drinking too much, and give each contestant the respect that they deserve for being on stage. Those are the qualities I would look for when seating a panel.

Stephanie Stuart

A judge need to be able to put everything aside, sit at the table stone-faced, and show no reaction to any of the competition to score accordingly.

Rico Taylor

Impractical, not one sided. Doesn't play favorites, gives everyone a fighting chance to earn a fair score, and everyone a equal shot. Don't judge if you feel you might be one-sided to a contestant.

Breonna Tenae

For a judge to be fair, is to know what every entertainer put into their package. Judge very objectively. Don't be the one looking to get every one for every thing. Look at the most important criteria to the system and the qualities needed to uphold the title. No favoritism. Judge each contestant as if you have never seen them before.

Tori Taylor

No matter how hard or easy a judge judges, they should look to each contestant equally.

Taina T Norell

A judge must know the true meaning of professionalism. Just because your sister is a contestant, doesn't mean your going to score her higher if she didn't deserve it. If you don't like a contestant from outside the competition, that's an issue.

Tiffani Middlesexx

Judges need to be impartial.

Jay Santana

A judge must be impartial. When judging a pageant, a judge has no friends on the stage. Objectivity must be maintained at all times. Judges should, not communicate with the contestants during a pageant.

Mykul Jay Valentine

Judges should be brought in from all over the country and not know anything about anyone competing. This way, they will have a unbiased opinion about anyone in the pageant.

Dana Douglas

A person who can put their personal preferences and friendships aside, to be impartial and open the overall, best performer in front of them that evening!

Jennifer Foxx

Most people hired to be judges in any kind of credible system, have already been screened by the system on a whole, so if you stand in a reputable system, the judges are certified.

Mis Sadistic

A fair judge is someone who is impartial, and with pageant experience. It should be someone who has been on that stage in the place where the hopefuls are standing being judged now. This to me makes for a fair judge.

Ty Nolan

Knowledge of the system. They are looking for...impartiality.

Freddy Prinze Charming

Impartial judges are a must. They should have no connection, either professional or personal to any of the contestants. They should not be connected to the pageant, either as a promoter or in any other capacity.

AJ Menendez

1. Understanding of the craft and what it entails. Understanding with firsthand knowledge what is expected in a competition. They should know what to look for in each category. 2. Don't be harsh. Write things like, "I would've liked to have seen" rather than, "You should have done this instead…"

Jayden Knight

They need to stay neutral to all contestants. No one should be partial to a certain person. They need somebody who has knowledge of the system.

Joey Jay

I bring in judges from out of town, so they have less of an opinion on the competitors. If it is their first time seeing a competitor, they are more likely to be truthful and give them honest advice.

Ty Nolan

Knowledge of the system. They are looking for…impartiality.

Natasha Richards

The ability to overlook any personal relationship with any contestant! The rules given must be abided by. Be professional and do your homework. Good lord, don't let them see you drink until after the pageant.

Gage Gatlyn

For a judge to be a fair judge, they must first be a good person, able to differentiate between business and personal, as well.

**"Ugliness is the stain of confusion
often left after the truth
washes away the lie."**
The Infamous Todd Kachinski Kottmeier

Chapter Fourteen

"Misconceptions" about competing in the pageantry systems"

UNEDITED RESPONSES

Bob Taylor

They are rigged or a system favors one type of entertainer over another.

Amy DeMilo

Just because you don't win, doesn't mean you weren't good. Just because you have a name doesn't mean you will win. It's all a bunch of smoke and mirrors.

Natasha Richards

You are the final ingredient in the recipe. You are going to hit that stage, they are not. Make it yours, no matter what. You have got to learn how to lose before you can win. Are you ready? Do not listen to everybody, take it all in then make your decision.

Dana Douglas

1. That they can be so fierce that they can break the rules. 2. That your name is enough to get you into the top five. 3. That once you win, your the "T" and you don't have to work hard anymore.

Brittany Moore

Not knowing what they are competing in and for...

Coco Montrese

Three top misconceptions is that, A. You are made for every system, B. My friends say I should've won C. The system should change to accommodate who I am as an entertainer.

Vinnie Marconi

1. The 'favorite' always wins. 2. The crowd loves what they do, so the judges will. 3. Winning the crown is just the BEGINNING of the hard work to come! You must "REPRESENT!

Denise Russell

Just because you don't win, does not mean that you are a bad performer. I know many great national performers that never competed. The best performer does not always win. Everyone can have a bad night.

Anson Reign

Just because you're the best King in your town and your home bar loves you don't mean you're going to be the best King at a pageant. Go with an open mind - anything can happen.

Vivika D'Angelo

Failure, discrimination, and lack of listening skills.

Sam Hare

(1) Their supporters are unbiased when telling them that they should have won if they did not, (2) All you have to be is pretty, OR talented, OR smart to win, and (3) You do not have to invest in yourself or believe in yourself to be successful. The biggest thing to watch in a system is who the promoter is seating on a panel. If they are not seating fair and competent judges do NOT waste your time and money. The judges' panel is vital to the success of a system.

Jay Santana

They are all fixed and the judges are paid for a desired outcome.

Stephanie Stuart

The pageant is a very stressful event! I refer to it sometimes as the twenty-four hours of drag because for those twelve hours before and the twelve hours after… you're totally focused on competition! Before you spend the time getting ready and obsessed after evaluating how it went

Rico Taylor

There all rigged or one sided if you can't dance you can't win or so and so is entering I have no chance pageant are meant to be fun learning experiences not one sided cheap shots remember the judges are there to help you grow as a individual and a performer some are harsh take it like a grain of salt and say thank you it wont always be like this promise read and grow from your judges comments

Breonna Tenae

Popularity doesn't win pageants only hard work and consistency. If the crowd loves you don't mean you win you have to convince the judges. Not all pageants are rigged" most are fair and square."

Tori Taylor

That it is a good way of getting bookings, it is a job! That it is a glamorous life, it is a job. That you will be more popular, again it is a job, it ends when you leave the venue, then you are alone in a strange hotel room with an early wake up call.

Taina T Norell

Some entertainer's don't take the art form serious enough. They come to this business for the wrong reasons Pageants are not a joke this is an art form that many entertainers across the nation takes very seriously

Mykul Jay Valentine

1. "They don't stand a chance at winning their first time out." That's not true. Anyone can win with the right package no matter who they are. 2. If you don't win, learn from your mistakes, change them, and come back next year bigger and better.

Jennifer Foxx

I think the primary misconception is, "I do not have enough behind me to win, not enough money, not this, or .not that." Anyone can win that is clean and consistent."

Ty Nolan

You do not win because who you are, but what you bring.

Jayden Knight

1. It is an easy win and it doesn't take much time, effort and money. 2. It is rigged, and the best contestant will win. 3. People are vicious.

Joey Jay

There is still work to do after you win. It is not just a free ride with a crown. You are the face of a system for a year, and people have expectations. Grow, Grow, And Grow.

Freddy Prinze Charming

That winning a crown gives you license to have an inflated ego. Competing is easy. Just because you have been performing for a few months, does not mean you are ready for the responsibility of the title.

AJ Menendez

A mistaken contestant believes no one can beat them. No matter your talent, there is always someone better than you. NEVER underestimate fellow contestants. Another mistake is having the belief if you happen to know one of the judges, it means an automatic win.

Mis Sadistic

One very big misconception about the pageant systems people make is they are not beauty pageants. They are looking for well rounded articulate talent. It is not just about looking pretty or looking the most real as a female.

Gage Gatlyn

The top misconception about Master MI is that it is a pageant. Master Male Illusionist is a high skill contest for Male

Illusionists. There is No Eveningwear, interview, Q&A, and judged presentation, Only Talent, Talent, Talent ...and Personality.

Darryl Kent

1. Everything will always be fair. 2. Just because you have won before with the same package, it does not make the package flawless. 3. A name is only a name, never read too much into a contestant list.

DRAG411's DRAG Memorial page on DRAG411.com

**"We cannot seek achievement for ourselves
and forget about progress and prosperity for our community...
Our ambitions must be broad enough to include the aspirations
and needs of others, for their sakes and for our own."**
Cesar Chavez

Chapter Fifteen

"After the Crown"

UNEDITED RESPONSES

Amy DeMilo

It hasn't changed my life. It was a goal I set and achieved, a magical moment, before returning back to reality.

DeyJzah Opulent Mirage

Each crown I won allowed me to grow in many ways. They pushed me to do other things across the country and increased my esteem. With each title, my assertiveness has increased thus my managerial skills have gotten even better than they were before. You reign is what you make it and I strive to make it a great thing for my drag life as well as my personal life

Brittany Moore

Gave me confidence to believe in myself. Gave me a platform to make a difference to help other contestants achieve their dreams.

Coco Montrese

Becoming Miss Gay America 2010 changed my life completely, I was discovered while on the road traveling as MGA2010 by the longest running headliner on the Las Vegas strip, he offered me a job on the spot to join his show once my reign was over and now I'm living the life I dreamed of in a show six nights a week on the famous Las Vegas strip.

Vinnie Marconi

I'm still taken aback by the recognition. In and out of face, people come up to me to say "aren't you...?" I carry a calender noting work, babysitting, and an occasional outings in it. NOW I look for those empty spots to just spend some time with my honey or friends! I can't even fathom how some people win crown after crown and hold multiple titles in the same year! I put so much work into the comparatively small titles I have, how can they possibly properly 'represent' them ALL?

Jennifer Foxx

Became the first female impersonator to appear on national television in 1981, with 60 television programs, over a 100 publications, a lecture tour across the USA, being a headliner in the casino industry as Mr. Joan Rivers (La Cage) for years and still working weekly to this day. The art of female impersonation as an actor has afforded me a living for now 35 years. I am very grateful. and honestly, very blessed.

Mis Sadistic

When I won the Miss Key West Pageant crown my life changed. I was able to have a platform to speak from, and an audience that would listen. I realized I was able to encourage people to go vote so we could get change in our community. Many doors opened, and seeing the other lives I am able to change. All from winning a crown.

Ty Nolan

Onstage, it gave me the desire to continue entertaining and competing. Offstage it gave me confidence, sense of accomplishment, and wonderful memories.

Freddy Prinze Charming

I was the first king west of Texas to win a title in a nationally recognized pageant, and it opened so many doors for me. It gave me an extra boost of confidence, both on and off the stage, and has put me in positions where I have been able to meet so many other entertainers.

Stephanie Stuart

It changed one thing and one thing only....CONFIDENCE! It made me confident and in return, I relaxed and settled in my position as an entertainer. When I see people enjoying what I was doing, I became a better person as well as an entertainer.

AJ Menendez

When I first competed for Boiling Point back in 2007, I competed as a Kitten (A female Performer). Yes, you read that correctly. I came in first alternate, but wanted to represent the title. I believed so very much in what it stands for. So, I worked hard at it. When I got the chance, I won it as a Male Illusionist. I had the honor of being crowned by my very own Drag Father, Wolfie. Boiling Point has become over the years, not just a title I hold, but my family. A family I can count on for anything. It's not just a national title to me. I owe my knowledge and my success as a Male Illusionist to the founder and members of Boiling Point. They have taught me the history of the craft and given me an amazing insight to being a Male Illusionist. They've taught me professionalism, technique, respect and helped me develop a passion for the craft I don't believe I would have been able to obtain anywhere else.

Denise Russell

I have enjoyed a very long career and the national pageants allowed me to start traveling all over the country. I made many great friends through the pageants. The hard work that it takes to compete, made me a better performer.

Jayden Knight

It made me start changing how I perform. It made me grow into a better performer. It made me well known on and off stage. It opened many doors for me as a performer.

Vivika D'Angelo

Changed me by making me a better person and made me more involved with the community along with not being scared of failing

Joey Jay

Say goodbye to your personal life. You may have to take a small hibernation from the partying and really get your job on.

Taina T Norell

It help me gained self confidence in myself in a territory I wasn't known.

Natasha Richards

Winning Miss Gay U.S. of A. at the age of twenty four enabled me to travel the country, meet some amazing people and financially made it possible for me to enjoy owning my own home, car and independence. It also helped surround me with great friends and family, there for allowing me to make a difference in our community, straight and gay. What more can someone ask for, "I will always be a Miss Gay U.S. of A."

Tiffani Middlesexx

Winning Miss Florida propelled my career in Florida.

Sam Hare

Having not won a crown, I cannot answer this as intended. However, I have worked with many national contest winners and winning on-stage is only the beginning. Having a successful reign takes motivation, dedication, hard work and patience. You will have to work a lot, push yourself, and realize that what you do with this title is helping to prepare for the next one. Be friendly, organized, and learn to compromise off-stage to be successful in the industry long-term. You are a brand so believe in the brand, push yourself and your support team, learn to sew and do hair and make-up and be a leader. Stay away from negativity and treat this as a business and you will be successful.

Mykul Jay Valentine

On stage, I am now getting booked more and people look up to me for advice and help, which I love because I love helping people. Nothing is better than seeing someone you helped succeed to achieve their dream of winning a title. I know what it feels like, and it feels amazing. Off stage, it's opened up so many opportunities, such as this one. Everyone will always remember who I am and everything I did for the system I represent. It always feels good to say, "I was a national title holder!"

Anastacia Dupree

Being a titleholder allows me to showcase my talent. It also helps me grow in the art and better my craft.

Rico Taylor

I feel like I have more confidence in myself and what I do and more respect for myself and from my Peers it let's me know all the talent nights hot spots and benefits weren't in vain and I finally became who I want to become.

Breonna Tenae

Winning a crown gave me more confidence in my ability to perform and entertain. It let me work in places I normally wouldn't and meet people and make new friends. Winning pageants and crown bolstered my career as a performer!

Darryl Kent

It gave me confidence to know I could stand tall among men half my size and half my age. I won Mr. Renaissance at 279 pounds and at the age of forty-six.

Tori Taylor

It let me know I had done the work. It made me the administrator for the system, responsible for not only my actions, but those representing the system.

Dana Douglas

Winning this title gave me back my confidence. It allowed me to have pride in my craft and encouraged me to be the best entertainer I can be. Not because I think I am the best, but I want my friends and my audience to say, "She's the Best!"

End of Book 3 of The 10 Black Books

Now, if this book
brought you any knowledge,
pass it on.

*Better yet, get them
their own copy!*

DRAG411.com

Ten Black Books

Ten Black Books

Book 1   DRAG411's
"DRAG Bully, A Survivor's Guide"

The Largest Bullying Project in LGBT History for Struggling Entertainers. Advice from over a hundred male, female, and androgynous impersonators around the world to help entertainers struggling with their family, peers, relationships, neighbors, regular jobs, venues, and successfully overcoming self-doubt. Best Selling author Todd Kachinski Kottmeier created DRAG411 to document the lives of male, female, and androgynous impersonator years ago. It is now the largest organization for impersonators on earth with over 7,000 entertainers in 32 countries. DRAG411 also operates The International Original, Official DRAG Memorial with almost a thousand names (2018). This is his 25th book, 20th World Record, and 12th book on this subject. Thousands of invitations to contribute were send out. This book contains the best of their responses, in their own words, to you.

Book 2 DRAG411's
"Original DRAG Handbook"

Over 155 female impersonators (and 1 male impersonator) from around the world share over a thousand insightful comments in the first handbook created of this art form.

Commentary shared with Todd Kachinski Kottmeier included the following contributors of The Original, DRAG Handbook to include Ada Buffet, Adora , Adrian Leigh, Afeelya Bunz, Alisa Summers, Alanna Divine, Alexis De La Mer, Alexis Mateo, Alex Serpa, Allure, Amanda Bone, Amanda Love, Amy DeMilo, Anastaia Fallon, Astasnaia Rexia, Angel gLamar, Angela Dodd, Anita Cox, April Fresh, Ashleigh Cooley, Aurora Sexton, Babette Schwartz, Bailey St. James, Barbra Herr, Barbra Seville, Beverly LaSalle, BJ Stephens, Blair Michaels, Brandon M. Caten, Brianna Lee, Brittany Moore, Brookyln Bisette, Bukkake Blaque London St. James, Cartier Paris, Cathy Craig, Champagne T. Bordeaux, Cherry Darling, Christina Paris, CoCo LaBelle, CoCo Montrese, CoCo St. James, Conundrum, Crystal Belle, Daniel Murphy, Danika Fierce, Daphne Ferraro, Dasha Nicole, Dee Gregory, Deva DaVyne, Diamond Dunhill, Diedra Windsor Walker, Dmentia Divinyl/Eva LaDeva, Echo Dazz, Esme Russell, Estelle Rivers, Eunyce Raye, Felica Fox, Felina Cashmere, Geraldine Queen Cabaret, Ginger Minj, Glitz Glam, Gilda Golden, Horchata, Ima Twat, Ineeda Twat, Jade Daniels, Jade Jolie, Jade Shanell, Jade Sotomayo, Jaeda Fuentes, Jami Micheals, Jay Santana, Jeffrey Powell, Jenna Chambers Tisdale, Jessica Jade, Jocelyn Summers, Jodie Holliday, Joey Brooks, Joshua Myers, J.P. Patrick, Juwanna Jackson, Kamden Wells, Katrina Starr, Kenny Braverman, Khrystal Leight, Kier Sarkesian, Kiki LaFlare Santangilo, Kitty D'Meaner, Kori Stevens, Krystal Amore Adonis, Lacey Lynn Taylors, Lady Clover Honey, Lady Sabrina, Lady TaJma Hall, Lakeisha Pryce, LeeAnna Love, Leigh Shannon, Lisa Carr, Lola Honey, Madisyn De

La Mer, Makayla Rose Devine, Maxine Padlock (Maxi Pad), Melissa Morgan, Melody Mayheim, Michael Wilson, Mike Astermon-Glidden, Mis Sadistic, Miss Conception, Miss Gigi, Mr. Kenneth Blake, Misty Eyez, Monique Michaels, Myah Monroe, Mystique Summers, Nairobi V. D'Viante, Naomi D-Lish, Naomi Wynters, Nicole Paige Brooks, Nikki Dynamite, Nova Starr, Ororo, Patrica Grand, Patricia Knight, Patrica Mason, Pandora DeStrange, Penelope Reigns, Polly FunkChanel, Phiore Star Liemont, Purrzsa Kyttyn, Pussy LeHoot, Raquel Payne, Rhyana Vorhman, Rickie Lee, Rusti Fawcett, Scarlett Fever, Selina Kyle, Shae Shae LaReese, Shealita Babay, Shugah Caine, Stephanie Roberts, Stephanie Stuart, Stormy Vain, Summer Breeze, Sybil Storm, Tabatha Lovall, Tatum Michelle, Teri Courtney, Tiffani Middlesexx, Timm McBride, Toni Davyne, TotiYanah Diamond,Trixie LaRue, Trixie Pleasures, Vegas Platinum, Venus D Lite, Vivika D'Angelo, Wendel Duppert and Wendy G. Kennedy.

Book 3:   DRAG411's
"Crown Me! Winning Pageants"

Hundreds of invitations sent to the titleholders, pageant promoters, judges, and talent show hosts to share their insight on not only winning pageants and contests but also owning the stage every time they perform. Their topics included auxiliary steps to success needed for song selection, dancing, movement on stage, props, backup dancers, creating your own edge, personal interviews, steps to success for winning the talent category every time you step on stage, on stage questions, eveningwear, and creative costuming. They discussed in their own unedited words, wardrobe changes, makeup, hair, shoes, when is the time to compete, qualities needed for a judge, and the top misconceptions of contestants competing in the pageantry systems.

Commentary shared with Todd Kachinski Kottmeier included the following contributors of Crown Me! to include AJ Menendez, Amy Demilo, Anastacia Dupree, Anson Reign, Bob Taylor, Breonna Tenae, Brittany T Moore, Coco Montrese, Dana Douglas, Darryl Kent, Denise Russell, Dey Jzah Opulent, Freddy Prinze Charming, Gage Gatlyn, Jay Santana , Jayden Knight, Jennifer Foxx, Joey Jay, Kori Stevens, Mis Sadistic, Mykul Jay Valentine, Natasha Richards, Rico Taylor, Sam Hare, Stephanie Stuart, Taina T. Norell, Tiffani Middlesexx, Tori Taylor, Ty Nolan, Vinnie Marconi, and Vivika D'Angelo.

Book 4:   DRAG411's
"DRAG King Guide"

Over 155 male impersonators around the world share over a thousand insightful comments in forty-one chapters.

Commentary shared with Todd Kachinski Kottmeier included the following contributors of The Official DRAG King and Male Impersonators Guide to include Aaron Phoenix, Abs Hart, Adam All, Adam DoEve, AJ Menendez, Alec Allnight, Alexander Cameron, Alik Muf, Andrew Citino, Anjie Swidergal, Anson Reign, Ashton The Adorable Lover, Atown, Ayden Layne, B J Armani, B J Bottoms, Bailey Saint James, Ben Doverr, Ben Eaten, Bootzy Edwards Collynz, Brandon KC Young-Taylor,

Bruno Diaz, Cage Masters, Campbell Reid Andrews, Chance Wise, Chandler J Hart, Chasin Love, Cherry Tyler Manhattan, Chris Mandingo, Clark Kunt, Clint Torres, Cody Wellch Klondyke, Colin Grey, Corey James Caster, Coti Blayne, Crash Bandikok, Dakota Rain, Dante Diamond, Davion Summers, DeVery Bess, Devin G. Dame, Devon Ayers, Dionysus W Khaos, Diseal Tanks Roberts, D-Luv Saviyon, Dominic Demornay, Dominic Von Strap, D-Rex, Dylan

Kane, E. M. Shaun, Eddie C. Broadway, Emilio, Erick LaRue, Flex Jonez, Freddy Prinze Charming, Gabe King, Gage Gatlyn, George De Micheal, Greyson Bolt, Gunner Gatlyn, Gus Magendor, Hawk Stuart, Harry Pi, Holden Michael, Howie Feltersnatch, Hurricane Savage, J Breezy St James, Jack E. Dickinson, Jack King, Jake Van Camp, Jamel Knight, Jenson C. Dean, Johnnie Blackheart, Jonah Godfather of DRAG, Jordan Allen, Jordan Reighn, Joshua K. Mann, Joshua Micheals, Juan Kerr, Julius M. SeizeHer, Jude Lawless, Justin Cider, Justin Luvan, Justin Sider, K'ne Cole, Kameo Dupree, Kenneth J. Squires, King Dante, King Ramsey, Jack Inman, Kody Sky, Koomah, Kristian Kyler, Kruz Mhee, Linda Hermann-Chasin, Luke Ateraz, Lyle Love-It, Macximus, Marcus Mayhem, Marty Brown, Master Cameron Eric Leon, Max Hardswell, MaXx Decco, Michael Christian, Mike Oxready, Miles Long, Mr-Charlie Smith, Nanette D'angelo Sylvan, Nolan Neptune, Orion Blaze Browne, Owlejandro Monroe, Papa Cherry, Papi Chulo, Papi Chulo Doll, Persian Prince, Phantom, Pierce Gabriel, Rasta Boi Punany, Rico M Taylor, Rock McGroyn, Rocky Valentino, Rogue DRAG King, Romeo Sanchez, Rychard "Alpha" Le'Sabre, Ryder Knightly, Ryder Long, Sam Masterson, Sammy Silver, Santana Romero, Scorpio, Shane Rebel Caine, Shook ByNature, Silk Steele Prince, SirMandingo Thatis, Smitty O'Toole, Soco Dupree, Spacee Kadett, Starr Masters, Stefan LeDude, Stefon Royce Iman, Stefon SanDiego, Stormm, Teddy Michael, Thug Passion, Travis Luvermore, Travis Hard, Trey C. Michaels, Trigger Montgomery, Tyler Manhattan, Viciouse Slick, Vinnie Marconi, Welland Dowd, William Vanity Matrix, Wulf Von Monroe, Xander Havoc, and Xavier Bottoms.

Book 5:   DRAG411's
"DRAG Stories"

Funny stories shared with Todd Kachinski Kottmeier including the following contributors of DRAG Stories to include Chance Wise, Anson Reign, Tiffani Middlesexx, Rico Taylor, Todd Kachinski Kottmeier, Bob Taylor, Stefon Royce Iman, Candi Samples, Alexis Mateo, Naomi Wynters, Dmentia Divinyl, Bruce Lacie, Kennedy Wendy, Chastity Rose, Miss GiGi, Angel gLamar, Patricia Grand, Shook ByNature, Lady Guy, Eunyce Raye, Charley Marie Coutora, Jezzie Bell, Lamar Kellam, Jayden St. James, Rachelle Ann Summers, Champagne T Bordeaux, Gilda Golden, Daisha Monet, Vivika D'Angelo, Rachel Boheme, Esme Rodriguez, and MaNu Da Original.

Book 6:   DRAG411's
"DRAG Mother, DRAG Father" Honoring Mentors

Performers look to DRAG mothers, DRAG fathers, friends, and fans for insight, compassion, and guidance as mentors. This book honors those special people. Over 140 entertainers contributed wisdom and words for this historical book, making it the largest project of its nature in GLBTQ history and the first published book on male and female mentors.

Commentary shared with Todd Kachinski Kottmeier included the following contributors of DRAG Parents to includee AJ Menendez, Vinnie Marconi, Mis Sadistic, Todd Kachinski Kottmeier, Bob Taylor, Taina Norell, Andrew Stratton, Horchata Horchata, David Warner, Gianna Love, Trinity Taylor, Domunique Jazmin Vizcaya, Brittany Moore, PurrZsa Kyttyn, Jake Lickus, Shelita Taylor, Adriana Manchez, MiMi Welch, China Taylor, Armondis Bone't, Monique Trudeau, Simeon Codfish, Diamond Dupree, Stefon Royce Iman, Jayden Stjames, Demonica da Bomb, Colin Grey, Christopher Todd Guy, Celyndra Lashay Clyne, Candice St. James, Justin Barnes Williams, Ivanna Dooche, London Taylor Douglas, Christina Alexandria Victoria Regina Lowe, Bianca DeMonet, Critiqa Mann, Jazmen Andrews, AJ Allen, TotiYanah Diamond, D' Marco Knight, Chip Matthews, Mirage Montrese, India Starr Simms, Jade S Stratton, Emerald Divine, Elysse Giovanni, Vanity Halston, Kristofer Reynolds, Akasha Uravitch, Adriana Fuentes, Erykah Mirage, Felicity Ferraro, Joey Payge, Rhiannon Todd, Vicious Slick, Amirage Saling, Tori Sass, Chy'enne Valentino, and Robbi Lynn.

Book 7:   DRAG411's
"Spotlight Today"

It was the World's Largest Paperback Magazine for Impersonators and Fans when it premiered with over 175 pages. DRAG411 no longer prints Spotlight Today Magazine, but here is the re-release of the groundbreaking first edition. Complete articles by Vinnie Marconi, Denise Russell, Tiffani T. Middlesexx, Kristofer Reynolds, Magenta Alexandria Dupree, Butch Daddy, Vivikah Kayson-Raye, Makanoe, Amanda Lay, Thomas DeVoyd, Kevin B. Reed, Glenn Storm, and over 150 impersonators from around the world.

Book 8:   DRAG411's
"DRAG Queen Guide"

Almost two hundred female impersonators around the world share over a thousand insightful comments in forty-one chapters.

Commentary shared with Todd Kachinski Kottmeier included the following contributors of Official DRAG Queen and Female Impersonator Handbook to include Alana Summers, Alexis Marie Von Furstenburg, Alize', Aloe Vera, Alysin Wonderland, Amanda Bone DeMornay, Amanda Lay, Amanda Roberts, Amy DeMilo, Anastasia Fallon, Angie Ovahness, Anita Mandinite, Appolonia Cruz, Ashlyn Tyler, Aurora Tr'Nele Michelle, Azia Sparks, Barbie Dayne, Barbra Herr, Beverly LaSalle, Bianca DeMonet, Bianca Lynn Breeze, Blair Michaels, Boxxa Vine, Brittany T Moore, Britney Towers, Brandi Amara Skyy, Brooke Lynn Bradshaw, Candi Samples, Candi Stratton, Candy Sugar, Cathy Craig, Catia Lee Love, CeCe Georgia, Cee-Cee LaRouge-Avalon, Celeste Starr, Chad Michaels, Chevon Davis, Cheyenne Desoto Mykels, Chi Chi Lalique, Christina Collins, Chrystal Conners, Claudia B Eautiful, Coca Mesa, Coco St James, Damiana LaRoux, Dana Scrumptious, Danyel Vasquez, Dee Gregory, Delores T. Van-Cartier, Demonica DaBaum, Denise Russell, Diamond Dunhill, Diva Lilo, Diva Savage, Dove, EdriAna Treviño, Elle Emenopé, Elysse Giovanni, Erica James, Esmé Rodríguez, Estella Sweet, Eunyce Raye, Eva Nichole Distruction, Faleasha Savage, Felicia Minor, Felicity Frockaccino, Gigi Masters, Ginger Alley, Ginger Gigi Diamond, Ginger Kaye Belmont, Glitz Glam, Grecia Montes D' Occa, Heather Daniels, Hennessy Heart, Hershae Chocolatae, Holy McGrail, Hope B Childs, Horchata, India Brooks, India Ferrah, Ivy Profen, Izzy Adahl, Jaclyn St James, Jade Iroq, Jade Sotomayor, Jade Taylor Stratton, Jamie-Ree Swan, Jennifer Warner, Jessica Brooks, Jexa Ren'ae Van de Kamp, Joey Brooks, Jonny Pride, Kamelle Toe, Karma Jayde Addams, Kelly Turner, Mama Savannah Georgia, Mr. Kenneth Blake, Kamden T. Rage, Kira Stone-St James, Kirby Kolby, Kita Rose, Krysta Radiance, Lacie Bruce, Lady Jasmine Michaels, Lady Pearl, Lady Sabrina, Latrice Royale, LaTonga Manchez, Leona Barr, Lexi Alexander, Lilo Monroe, Lindsay Carlton, Lucinda Holliday, Lunara Sky, Lupita Chiquita Michaels Alexander, Madam Diva Divine, Mahog Anny, Makayla Michelle Davis Diamond, Mariah Cherry, Maxine Padlock, Melody Mayheim, Menaje E'toi, Mercede Andrews, Mi$hal, Mia Fierce, Michelle Leigh Sterling, Miss Diva Savage, Miss GiGi, Misty Eyez, Mitze Peterbilt, Monica Mystique, Montrese Lamar Hollar, Morgana DeRaven, Muffy Vanbeaverhousen, Natasha Richards, Nathan Loveland, Nicole Paige Brooks, Nikki Garcia, Nostalgia Todd Ronin, Olivia St James, Paige Sinclair, Pandora DeCeption, Pheobe

James, Reia'Cheille Lucious, Robyn Demornay, Robyn Graves, Rhonda Sheer, Rose Murphy, Ruby Diamond NY, Ruby Holiday, Ryan Royale, Rychard "Alpha" Le'Sabre, Rye Seronie, Sable Monay, Sabrina Kayson-Raye, Samantha St Clair, Sanaa Raelynn, Sapphire T. Mylan, Sasha Phillips, Savannah Rivers, Savannah Stevens, Selina Kyle, Sha'day Halston-St James, ShaeShae LaReese, Shamya Banx, Shana Nicole, Shaunna Rai, Sierra Foxx White, Sierra Santana, Sonja Jae Savage, Stella D'oro, Strawberry Whip, Sugarpill, Tasha Carter, Tanna Blake, Taquella Roze, Tawdri Hipburn, Taylor Rockland, Tempest DuJour, Tiffani T. Middlesexx, Traci Russell, Trudy Tyler, Vanessa del Rey, Velveeta WhoreMel, Vera Delmar, Vicky Summers, Vita DeVine, Vivian Sorensin, Vivian Von Brokenhymen, Vivika D'Angelo-Steele, Wendy G. Kennedy, Willmuh Dickfit, Wynter Storm, Yasmine Alexander and ZuZu Bella.

Book 9:   DRAG411's (Two Comedy Scripts)
"Best Said Dead" and **"Following Wynter"**

Best Said Dead examines in funny conversations those brief minutes after a person dies. Many religions and beliefs define different paths for each of us. Rarely do we discuss those precious moments between death and the final destination. This comedy opens the possibilities that for a moment, a person vanishes into the memories in their mind. Any part can be male, female, or ambiguous.

Following Wynter is a hilarious comedy play. Ethan discovers his newlywed husband is the flamboyant DRAG queen Wynter Storm in this whimsical farce with an important message of believing in yourself and your friends. . . even if your friend is Serena Silver. Any part can be male, female, or ambiguous.

Book 10:   DRAG411's
"DRAG World"
The contributing writers of DRAG411's "Spotlight Magazine," the World's Largest Paperback Magazine for Impersonators and Fans when it premiered in 2012 with over 175 pages, created this companion book. DRAG411 no longer prints Spotlight Today Magazine, but above you will find Book 7 is the re-release of the groundbreaking first edition. Complete chapters on DRAG Marketing by DRAG411.

Complimentary articles on Confidence, Duct Tape, Music Selection, Living Divinely, authentic stage presence, Pageants, having fun performing, jewelry, legislative information from the United States and around the world,   the Old School performers, Virgin stage performers, and payday from contributing writers including Denise Russell, Jay Santana, Chance Wise, Vivikah Kayson-Raye, AJ Menedez, Glenn Storm, Freddy Prinze Charming, Gage Gatlyn, Kevin B. Reed, and over 100 impersonators from around the world!

Other books from the Best Selling **author
The Infamous Todd Kachinski Kottmeier**

Other books from the Best Selling author
The Infamous Todd Kachinski Kottmeier

"Turn Around Bright Eyes, The DRAG Queen Killer"

Few crimes in gay history rocked a nation as great as The DRAG Queen Killer. The country seemed paralyzed from the first ring of the chain tapping on the concrete, as they pulled Cassandra to her death, until the very last brutal killing. The murderous rampage seemed buried amongst the media suffering from a barrage of tales from the 9-11 terrorist attacks.

"CommUnity of Transition"

We sent over a thousand invitations to the transgender community around the world asking them to share wisdom, advice, and compassion for those questioning or struggling. No restraints, using topics they created, as they guided the conversation over forty chapters and fifty topics. By the close, these remarkable people had created the largest compilation book in transgender history. They opened their heart with these words.

NOTE: *This book is "lightly edited" to reflect the intent and form of over one hundred transgender contributors. Unedited photographs "before and after" come from actual contributing transgender writers.*

"Joey Brooks, The Show Must Go On"
By Joey Brooks and Todd Kachinski Kottmeier

Joey Brooks, The Show Must Go On is the story of The First Lady of Ybor from the days of El Goya to present day. Female Impersonator, Show director, hostess, author...
"Old school, new school, no school... who gives a shit? I'm too old to go to school. I barely remember last week. When I get too old to remember what the fuck I did when I was young ...ger, I'll just open one of these books and laugh my ass off. I wonder how many other queens had this much fun becoming one of the icons of their community. Too funny. I just called myself an icon. Hell, I must be a queen. Only a female impersonator could call themselves a diva, a queen, a star without people giggling behind her back. Giggling is good. A twenty-dollar bill is better."

"Two Days Past Dead"

The Author's First Published Book

It is hard to be the good guy when you succeed so well being bad. This is the Auggie Summer's dilemma his entire life. The story, based loosely on the tales of The Infamous Todd, follows the precocious child. His story begins with selling candy in 9th grade where he catches not only the attention of the press but also amusement of the drug cartel early in its' own infancy. Auggie Summers finds himself in the forefront of one of the most dangerous organizations on Earth.

"Waiting On God"
The Author's Humorist Novel

Learn to live after the doctors tell you "that are dying." A humorist essay on embracing funny moments and to create an environment around you that makes people not only laugh, but also be inspired by your strength.

www.ingramcontent.com/pod-product-compliance
Lightning Source LLC
Chambersburg PA
CBHW070129260726
48658CB00001B/331